The Guru'Guay Guide to Montevideo

Karen A Higgs

2016

GURU'GUAY

Guru'Guay Productions
Montevideo, Uruguay

IMPORTANT

The Guru'Guay website and guides to Uruguay & Montevideo
are an independent initiative.

Thanks for sharing the love and buying this guide.

For more check out the Guru'Guay website www.guruguay.com.

The Guru'Guay Guide to Montevideo is my first travel guide.
In 2016 I will be working on *The Guru'Guay Guide to Uruguay*.
I also have plans for Guru'Guay t-shirts! You want one already, right?

Looking forward to helping make your stay in
Montevideo and Uruguay really, really memorable

– Karen, aka "The Guru"

PS. I'd love to hear from you. See you on the site, Facebook or Twitter

To Sergio, the man behind the Guru

To my old friend Lesley Davies-Evans, who came up with the name Guru'Guay.
I love it, though the mantel weighs heavy

"Montevideo is a city whose charms are not at first obvious but which soon reveal themselves given the chance. Often seen as a side trip of a couple of days from Buenos Aires, Montevideo is worth much more than that. The city boasts one of the best collections of art-deco buildings anywhere in the world, has a lively arts scene including a great theatre and live music programme, eclectic cafes and restaurants and some interesting museums - most of which are free to visit. But perhaps the city's best assets are its 25 kilometres of promenade water front and its exceptionally friendly people." – Adrian Yekkes

"I was blown away by Montevideo. It has that bohemian, artsy vibe that I love about San Telmo (the old tango neighbourhood of Buenos Aires) but you feel like you are in a beach town. I'd been through the city a number of times on my way to the beaches further east, but I'd never actually spent any time there. Big mistake.

What a charming city, especially if you have spent time in hectic Buenos Aires. It's calmer, more laid back, and they take advantage of the river! In Montevideo, we saw kite surfers and families along the river's beaches, people heading to the bars and cafes near the river to take in the sunset, and the massive rambla is perfect for cycling, roller-blading, getting in a run or just walking off all of the fabulous food and drink." – Angela, San Telmo Loft

"I never thought I'd love Montevideo so much.
I mean, I've never even heard of this little capital city until a few months ago.

I was a little apprehensive about coming here after a not-so-welcoming experience in BA. I was afraid that maybe since these cities are so close to each other, they would be just the same. Turns out, I couldn't have been further from the truth. It's true that there are a lot of similarities in that both are heavily European-influenced cultures and have somewhat similar cuisines, but they may as well be on completely different continents.

Montevideo is seriously cool, but I feel like it's so overlooked.
Most people seem to think that it's only worth a few days of your time. Our BA hosts thought we were CRAZY to be spending a month here. Because it's small and boring, she said.
But though I've been here for almost three weeks now, I feel slightly panicked that I'll be leaving next week and won't see and do everything I want to." – Anna, Slightly Astray

Introduction from the Guru

A lot of people ask, how long should I visit Montevideo for? Well, **Montevideo has it all** – sun, sand, the world's longest carnival, progressive political system, amazing music and culture, a fifteen-mile promenade, ten beaches, more art-deco architecture than any city other than New York, historic cafes, great wine, great meat…

And as a **capital city** with just **one and a half million inhabitants**, Montevideo has all the features of a major city -an international airport, lots of cultural events, good public transport – yet it is small enough to get around easily even on foot and the locals are extremely friendly, the same as you would find in any small town.

There are **so many things to do** that it's **well-worth spending at least four nights** to really get a flavour of the city, though **I'd recommend staying a week or ten days** to be able to do day trips – and sleep a lot of siestas, because you're going to want to dive into the local live music scene and shows won't start till 10 pm.

Everything you'll read here is based on **my personal experience** and on comments and suggestions from the amazing guests from all over the world that who've come to stay at Casa Sarandi, the art-deco guesthouse my partner and I run in the Ciudad Vieja (Old City).

I actually started Guru'Guay because our guests complained it was virtually impossible to find a good guidebook on Uruguay. I later discovered why. Those guidebooks published by the big companies are written by people who fly in for a week and then leave.

I'm British but I've been living in Latin America for more than half my life. I moved to Montevideo in 2000. I'm also a professional **musician**, so I have close ties to music and culture here. *The Guru'Guay Guide to Montevideo* has been written on the basis of my experience of **fifteen years living right here** in the city.

The secret delights of Montevideo are not evident, not even if you speak Spanish. Use the guide, together with the Guru'Guay website and the Guru'Guay page on Facebook where I post **daily recommendations** of things to do in the evenings in Montevideo, and you'll have access to bang **up-to-date, insider information** while you are here.

For now, **Montevideo remains a unique off-the-radar destination on the South American circuit**. Lucky you. — *Karen A Higgs, aka "The Guru"*

Table of Contents

LOGISTICS

Logistics

Getting to and from Montevideo

Montevideo is in the centre of Uruguay on the southern coast. Of course you can fly to Montevideo, but you can also get here overland by bus from southern Brazil and different parts of Argentina and by ferry from Buenos Aires.

Remember that you cannot drive rental vehicles across international borders in South America.

From Argentina

From Buenos Aires direct to Montevideo

Ferry The most common way that people come from Buenos Aires is by direct ferry to Montevideo (2.25 hours), or by ferry/bus combo via Colonia (takes 4.5 to 5 hours in total).

Flying Flying from Buenos Aires to Montevideo takes just 40 minutes but I don't recommend it.

Bus General Belgrano runs an overnight bus service from Buenos Aires to Montevideo which runs daily and takes 8 hours.

From Buenos Aires to Montevideo with stop-offs

Via Colonia From Buenos Aires, you can take a direct ferry to Colonia (1 hr) and spend the day or longer there. The ferry companies do not allow you to make a stop-off, so just buy a ticket to Colonia. When you get off at the port, go to the bus station next door, buy a ticket to Montevideo for later in the day (you can see the old part of Colonia in 4-5 hours) and leave your bags in the left-luggage deposit for a small fee. The bus ride to Montevideo takes approx. 2.5 hours.

Via Carmelo A lesser-known option is the picturesque daily ferry from the Tigre Delta in Buenos Aires to Carmelo (wine country!) in Uruguay. The Tigre ferry company Cacciola has a website in Spanish only.

From the Argentina interior
Overnight buses run several times a week from Mendoza, Cordoba and Rosario to Montevideo. It may seem like a long trip, but the buses are very comfortable with sleeper beds and it's actually not

a bad way to get to Montevideo. Bus companies are EGA and Encon.

From Brazil

Flying From Rio and São Paulo, you are likely to want to fly. It takes 2.75 hours to fly from São Paulo and Rio de Janeiro to Montevideo. From southern Brazil (Rio Grande do Sul) it is a one-hour flight.

Bus Porto Alegre, the Brazilian city nearest the Uruguayan border, is a a 10-hour bus journey away. To be honest the price difference between flying and the bus is usually negligible, and so I would tend to recommend the one-hour flight. Bus companies are EGA and TTL.

Driving I do not recommend driving to Uruguay from Porto Alegre. Rental companies will not allow you to cross borders (this is the same for Argentina). In addition, the route from Porto Alegre to Chuy on the Uruguayan border goes through fairly uninspiring countryside and is a two-lane road crowded with enormous produce-filled juggernauts. It makes for extremely stressful driving.

From Europe, North America and the rest of the world
Of course you will have to fly. See *Airlines*

From the Iguazú Falls
There is a 24-hour bus from Iguazú to Montevideo. There are no direct flights to Uruguay. You have to fly via Argentina or Brazil. See *Airlines*

Time differences
If you are travelling the continent you should read about the time zone differences between Uruguay and the rest of South America. Since October 2015, there is no longer a difference in time between Buenos Aires and Uruguay as neither is currently observing daylight saving.

More reading on Guru'Guay.com
To choose what's best for you, I recommend you read my article on the different options for getting to Uruguay from Argentina[1] and why I don't recommend flying.
Having trouble using those ferry sites to find prices? They are impossible! I've produced a little matrix on ferry prices[2] which I will update periodically.

---

1   http://guruguay.com/what-is-the-best-way-to-travel-from-buenos-aires-to-montevideo/
2   http://guruguay.com/much-montevideo-buenos-aires-ferry-cost/

Flying to Montevideo

All airlines flying internationally into Uruguay fly to Montevideo's Carrasco airport about 15 miles (24 km) to the east of the city.

You'll have a choice of several carriers and I have a number of recommendations based on an analysis that is entirely non-scientific but that you will find useful. The analysis is based on my observation of the arrival times and luggage status of the folks who fly into Montevideo from all over the world each month and stay at my guest-house, the relative state of ire of my airport transfer guy who spends his week ferrying those passengers from Montevideo airport, exchanges with a bunch of peers here in Uruguay, and personal travel back and forth from Europe, the US and South Africa to Montevideo over the last 15 years.

Airlines flying from the US and Canada

American Airlines is the only airline to offer direct flights from the US to Uruguay. However, airline staff have confirmed to me off-the-record that American reserves its crappiest planes for these long-haul trips. And it is not sooo unusual for them to cancel the flight down.

Instead **consider using good Latin American airlines** like LAN Chile, Avianca and COPA.

Fellow travellers have told me that they have more leg room than the US airlines and have individual movie screens. This is an important detail when flights are long. **Avianca** and **Copa** are usually the cheapest. A flight with connections may only take a couple of hours longer than a direct flight (11.5 hours vs 9.5 hours for the direct flight).

While **transfers** in some airports can be a bit of a nightmare, especially when you don't speak the language, changing planes in Santiago (LAN), Panama City (COPA) and Lima (with Avianca) is a relative breeze.

Airlines flying from Europe

There are few direct flights from Europe to Uruguay and you will usually have to go through Buenos Aires or São Paulo.

- **I love TAM and LAN (to be rebranded as one airline LATAM by 2018)** Brazilian TAM and Chilean LAN fly newer planes with individual TV screens. They also allow you two suitcases for no extra charge. Currently you will fly on a TAM codeshare but I recommend booking through LAN as their zippy website is really usable and makes it very easy to identify the cheapest prices. Flights from London come through Madrid and Brazil and can take around 16-17 hours at their fastest.
- **Air Europa** is often significantly cheaper than the rest. Here in Montevideo I called them on a local line and got to speak to a very helpful human being immediately. And there is no extra charge for booking

over the phone. Based in Spain, a flight to Montevideo starting in Valencia was actually as cheap as coming from Madrid.

- **Air France** I haven't used them but a travel agent told me they have way better customer service than the other airlines. Think about using them if you are likely to have to alter your ticket.
- **Iberia** Uggh... Like the US airlines, Iberia seems to reserve its crappiest planes for these long distance flights while charging top dollar. Is it because we South Americans are a captive – and colonial – audience?

Is it best to fly to Montevideo via Argentina or Brazil?

My preference is through Brazil, especially now that the São Paulo airport has been modernised. Flying via Argentina from Europe means you are actually adding time to your trip as you effectively fly past Uruguay on the way to Argentina, and have to fly "back" again. But it's not really a huge difference.

Airlines flying from Argentina

Aerolineas Argentinas are a nightmare. The driver I use to pick up guests at the airport has come close to telling me that he won't pick up people flying in on Aerolineas any more as he is so tired of them being late and/or cancelling flights. If you can avoid them, do!

Coming from Buenos Aires, if you don't have much time, I would invariably take the ferry over flying.

Important note Buenos Aires has two airports – the Buenos Aires international airport known as Ezeiza (EZE) which is outside of the capital, and the national airport Aeroparque (AEP) which is in the city centre itself. If you are intent on flying from BA to Montevideo, unless you are already at Ezeiza, then save yourself time and money by getting your flight from Aeroparque.

Airlines flying from the Iguazú Falls

Unfortunately there are no direct flights to and from Uruguay currently. Flights with connections from Montevideo to Iguazú go via Buenos Aires (Aerolineas Argentinas) and São Paulo (TAM). With reasonable connections it's likely to take you about 6 hours to fly from Iguazú to Montevideo.

If you are on holiday and looking to relax, **I'd recommend staying overnight in Buenos Aires** to break up the trip and then flying on to Iguazú next day. The flight takes just under two hours. Then you can choose other options like **LAN** which flies three times a day from Aeroparque in the city centre.

Remember if you are from the US, Canada or Australia and entering Argentina even for a day trip to the falls, there is a 160 USD reciprocity fee that needs to be paid in advance (the good news is that the permit is valid for 10 years).

Airlines flying from Brazil

Direct flights are available from São Paulo, Porto Alegre and occasionally from Rio de Janeiro. Choose from TAM and Brazilian company GOL.

Airlines flying from other Latin American countries

There are direct flights from Chile, Panama, Peru, Paraguay and Bolivia. Fly from Panama with COPA, Lima (Peru) with Avianca, Santa Cruz (Bolivia) with Amaszonas, and Asunción (Paraguay) with BQB (note: this airline is currently negotiating its sale to Amaszonas). The excellent LAN flies from Chile of course. Beware, with the exception of the Bolivian flight and LAN, all the others land in the early hours of the morning.

A new Uruguayan airline

The state-supported national airline, Pluna, closed down several years ago, leaving a bunch of direct routes uncovered. A new venture run by ex-Pluna employees, the unfortunately-named Alas Uruguay – it stands for "Uruguay wings", before you ask – or Alas-U, will be flying to Montevideo from Buenos Aires, Santiago de Chile, Rio, São Paulo and Asunción. The airline intends to eventually run routes to Curitiba, Santa Cruz de la Sierra, Cordoba, Lima and Caracas (possibly by the end of 2016).

Getting to/from the airport, port or bus terminal

The port and bus station are in the centre of Montevideo. The airport is a 30-minute drive out to the east.

Getting to/from the port

The port is **located in the Old City** (Ciudad Vieja), so it's very central – just a five minute cab ride from Centro and 15 minutes from Pocitos and Punta Carretas. Cabs are plentiful. If you are staying in the Old City, you could walk unless you have a suitcase (uneven pavements make rolling difficult) or arrive after dark (like port areas around the world, it can be dodgy after dark).

Beware, unfortunately a number of taxi drivers from the port have tried to overcharge my guests whereas from the bus station this almost never happens – very odd. I recommend you ask your hotel how much your ride should cost, and check with the driver how much the trip is likely to cost before you get into the cab. If you do not feel confident to do this in Spanish beforehand and once you get to the hotel the driver tries to charge you more, tell him to wait and go into the hotel for assistance.

Getting to/from Montevideo's central bus station

The **bus terminal Tres Cruces**, where all long-distance buses arrive into Montevideo, is in the Tres Cruces neighbourhood, and about the same distances as above. You are walking distance to hotels in Centro and 15 minutes from Pocitos and Punta Carretas by cab.

The bus terminal is in the lower floor of a large shopping centre. The bus station has a decent cafeteria-style restaurant, a post office and facilities to charge your cell-phone. There is a taxi rank at the bus station. If the line is unbearably long, leave the station and flag down a cab outside.

Getting to/from the airport

The **airport is 15 miles** (apx 25 km) from the centre of Montevideo, a 30-40 minute cab ride into town depending on where you are staying. Traffic is very rarely a problem, but calculate a few minutes more around rush-hour or at the start of a long weekend.

You have a number of options for getting into Montevideo city centre from the airport.

To give you an idea of prices, I'll quote prices for November 2015 from the airport to the Old City, which is the longest trip to any central neighbourhood – about 40 minutes.

- **Remises** The most convenient, especially if you want to make use of every minute of your stay, is to have a private car waiting for you. These private cars are known as remises (reh-MEES). Your hotel can usually arrange a remise for you. A reasonable price for a remise to the Old City is about 1100 pesos.
- **Local buses** The cheapest is by local bus to Tres Cruces but only appropriate if you have little luggage, as buses get very full and have no storage areas. The bus stop is right outside the airport building and goes to the centre of Montevideo. The bus costs 51 pesos (December 2015). Catch any bus that says 'Montevideo'. The ride will take about one hour. Most buses come into Montevideo along Av Italia and then take Uruguay until the Rio Branco bus station close to the Plaza de Independencia. Keep your eye out for the Tres Cruces bus terminal if you intend to get off there – the bus doesn't actually stop in the terminal, but just outside. If you are heading to/from Punta Carretas take the DM1 bus which stops at the Punta Carretas, Montevideo and Portones shopping centres on the way. Buses run very frequently, even on weekends.
- **Airport shuttles** are also cheap – 350 pesos per person. They can be time-consuming if the other passengers are dropped off before you. Shuttles go once they have five passengers.
- **Airport taxis** The most expensive are the airport cabs – big silver sedans parked at the entrance. To the Old City, the cost is 1420 pesos. The prices are online[3].
- **Taxis** If you are going somewhere close to the airport you could call a regular cab using the number 1771 (Punta Gorda cabs). I don't advise it for longer trips as the costs will be similar to a remise and it will be much less comfortable.

---

3   http://www.taxisaeropuerto.com/tarifas.html

Weather and what to wear

Uruguay is a temperate country and there are four seasons:

Spring September, October, November
Summer December, January, February
Autumn March, April, May
Winter June, July, August.

Summer (December–February)

High season is short and includes the hottest months temperature wise – January and February. There can be occasional periods of rain and cloud at any point during the summer, which in my experience may last up to four days. But then the sun will come out and dry everything up.

In this period you must be really careful to **protect yourself from the sun**. Between November and March, if you go out at midday for more than 15 minutes without sunscreen on, <u>you are going to get burned</u>[4]. Uruguay, Argentina and Chile are perilously close to a big hole in the ozone layer and it's extremely easy to ruin your holiday on the very first day if you go out without sunscreen and a hat.

Spring and Autumn

Autumn (March-May) and **Spring** (September-November) are particularly lovely times weather-wise. Days are mild, around 20°C (68°F), and there are frequent Indian summers. **Nights** can be chilly from March on so bring layers. In fact, always plan to bring layers regardless of the season.

---

4   http://guruguay.com/sunbathing-in-uruguay-or-how-not-to-ruin-your-holiday/

Winter (June–August)

The average winter temperature is 15°C (59°F) during the day and rarely goes below zero at night in the city. Sounds wonderfully mild, right? But it might not be quite what you expect. A friend from Calgary in Canada (think MINUS 30°C, that's -22°F, in winter) came to stay in August. She later confessed that she had never felt as cold as she did during that winter in Montevideo.

Over a decade living here tells me that this is down to visitors from the Northern Hemisphere looking at the temperatures for June to August (winter in the Southern Hemisphere) and not preparing for coastal Uruguay's bone-penetrating **humidity** (read damp). They see 15°C and think.. sandals!

Saying that, winter can be exhilarating. There are periodic Indian summers. Sun-traps are easy to find. The days may feel very cold but they are usually gorgeously sunny. Even during the coldest months of July and August, the average sunlight hours are typically 6-7 hours a day. It's rare to have rain for more than a few days in a row.

Why does it feel so cold? Jules Verne was reporting on the wicked Pampero wind back in 1868. It's a polar front from the South Atlantic which affects Argentina, Uruguay and southern Brazil in the South's winter months. In Uruguay we mostly feel its effects on the temperature more than the wind itself. It feels so cold because it is so damp because of our being right on the vast River Plate and close to the Atlantic Ocean.

What to wear in winter

These are my essential tips to dressing to enjoy Montevideo in the winter. Follow them and avoid the sniffles.

- Layers, layers, layers – the sun comes out, you boil, the sun goes in, you are suddenly freezing again. Choose several layers instead of one thick one. If you wear one thick one, when the sun comes out you boil. And then you will end up taking that off and you will catch a cold.
- Warm footwear, especially boots, and gloves.
- Hats and wind-breakers – combat that wicked Pampero should it blow.

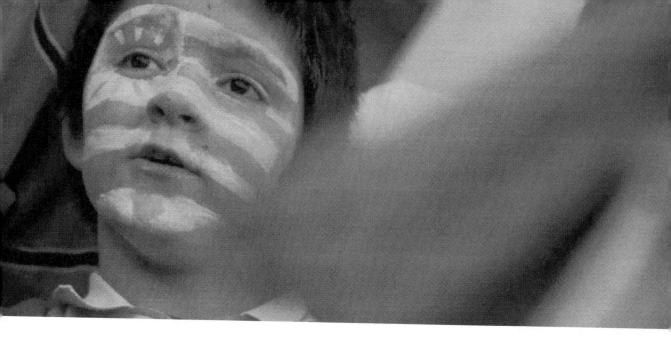

When is the best time to visit?

All year round. Montevideo, despite its small size for a capital city, has dozens of cultural events on every week, many of them free of charge.

Well, Montevideo has it all – sun, sand, a historically progressive political system, the world's longest carnival, tango venues that are NOT for export, historic cafes, great food, award-winning wines… As a capital city, Montevideo has an international airport, world-class entertainment and yet as it is so small it is easy to get around on foot or by bus and the people are extremely friendly to travellers.

There are so many things to do that it's worth spending at least four nights and ideally more to really get a flavour of the city. Or stay for ten days or more and do some day trips.

Planning your trip

Everyone has different ideas of what makes a perfect holiday, so here's a little matrix to help your planning. The initial of each month starting with January is at the top. So you can see that if you want hot weather, cheaper hotels and see a bit of carnival, your best bet is the start of March.

Best time to visit

	J	F	M	A	M	J	J	A	S	O	N	D
Music & culture	x*	x	x	x	x	x	x	x	x	x	x	x±
Soccer		x	x	x	x	x	x	x	x	x	x	
Hot weather	x	x	x							x	x	x
Carnival	x*	x	x									
Gorgeous spring & fall days			x	x	x				x	x	x	
Lowest hotel prices			x	x	x	x			x	x	x	
Cold but Indian summers						x	x	x	x	x		

* Starts last week of January
± Until Xmas Eve

GURU'GUAY

A few additional tips to keep in mind when planning your stay:

- **Weather** Uruguay has four seasons. Summer is from January to March, winter from May to August. January can be extremely hot. Winter is never very cold but it can be windy and damp so layers are essential. Spring and Autumn are very pleasant with mild temperatures. It never rains very much but it can rain at the height of summer for several days if you are unlucky.
- **Montevideo has numerous beaches** and 25 wonderful kilometres of unbroken **rambla** (promenade) good for **walking, running and cycling** all year round.
- **Beaches are good for swimming and sunbathing from November until April** and even occasional days the rest of the year.
- **The** Old City is best visited at its bustling best on weekdays. If you plan a four-night stay, make sure you arrive Thursday lunch-time at the latest.
- **The most interesting market** is Tristan Narvaja on Sunday mornings.
- **You can experience carnival throughout the year.** The official carnival season lasts a minimum 40 nights from the last week of January, throughout February to approximately the first week in March. It is not necessary to coincide with the parades to see the best of carnival – the *tablado* are really great.

- **Montevideo has many world-class live music events** any night of the week especially between March and up to the Christmas holidays. There is more choice Thursday to Saturday.
- **Museums and galleries** are usually free to enter but do not have much signage in English. Many museums only open Monday to Friday whereas art museums and galleries tend to open on weekends.
- **Montevideans take their public holidays seriously.** For instance, between Christmas and the New Year, many bars and restaurants are closed. January, especially the first two weeks, is also very quiet. Enjoy the peace and go to the beach, walk or cycle the rambla and make day trips. Then Carnival starts usually around the last week of January, and Montevideo's intense cultural activity is back on again.

Public holidays in Uruguay

Montevideans prioritise family life over business, so it's a good idea to know when public holidays are, as most shops except for shopping centres will close and local public transport runs on a limited schedule. Fortunately, as public transport is much better than in many countries, this shouldn't really affect you. Beaches will also be busier.

Public holidays when most shops and restaurants close (known here as "no-laborables")
January 1, May 1, July 18, August 25 and December 25. See Guru'Guay on Christmas and New Year in Montevideo[5]

Public holidays where many shops and restaurants remain open (known as "laborables")
January 6, April 19, May 18, June 19, October 12 and November 2

Other major public holidays are Carnival (two days in February, though most shops in Montevideo will close for the entire week) and Tourism Week (which coincides with Easter – Uruguay has complete separation of church and state[6]).

Why does the tourist industry in Montevideo close down at peak times?

Clients sometimes ask me this when I am suggesting they spend their New Years Eve eating left-overs and watching the fireworks from our building rooftop.

For a city that is a major tourist destination Montevideo can appear to have a pretty lame attitude to serving its guests over the holidays.
The biggest irony for me is that during Easter, one of the holidays where we receive waves of tourists from all over Latin America, there will be a huge sign across the front door of the government-run tourist information centre saying "Closed for Tourism Week". This year I'll take a picture.

After all this time living here, the conclusion that I have come to, is that the majority of Uruguayans are just not that materialistic. They would rather spend time with their family and friends than make a bit of extra money for working a holiday. Hence restaurants close because they just can't get the staff.

On one hand, being involved in the travel trade, it's really frustrating. On the other hand, I can't help thinking, a nation that prioritises its leisure time over making a buck is not so bad.

---

5   http://guruguay.com/montevideo-new-years-eve-christmas/
6   http://guruguay.com/why-uruguayans-celebrate-tourism-week-not-easter/

Holidays and festivals in Montevideo

An important word of warning. The date of celebrations changes year by year and festival dates are rarely confirmed more than a few weeks in advance. So please, please treat this list lightly as you plan your holiday. Guru'Guay can accept no responsibilities for date accuracy – I've done my best!

Dates marked * are from 2015, as 2016 dates are currently unavailable.

JANUARY

1 New Year
6 Children's Day though everyone calls it "Día de Reyes"
6 Llamadas de San Baltasar, Palermo Classic pre-carnival drumming and dance procession
6 Grand José Pedro Ramírez Horse-racing Cup, Maroñas Race-track See *Outdoors*
23 Carnival 2016 Parade (*desfile*), Centro down 18 de Julio Avenue See *Carnival*
25 Carnival shows (*tablados*) begin city-wide for the next 40 nights plus rain-checks

FEBRUARY

2 Iemanjá Sea Goddess celebrations, Parque Rodó See <u>Guru'Guay on Iemanjá</u>[7]
4 and 5 Llamadas Parade, Palermo
12-15* Festival de Tango Internacional, Radisson Hotel, Centro
All month long - Carnival shows (*tablados*)

---

7   http://guruguay.com/uruguay-festivals-celebrations-yemanja/

MARCH

Carnival ends *Tablados* usually still continuing for the first few days of the month

12* Vineyard Harvest Festival (Festival de la Vendimia) in associated vineyards in Montevideo and surrounding areas

Tourism Week

Gaucho Week (Semana Criolla Patria Grande), Rural del Prado Agricultural fair with gaucho rodeos and evening concerts during Easter. First edition in 1925.

APRIL

10-18* La Cumparsita Tango Week In honour of the world's most famous tango song. 2017 will be the 100th Anniversary. See <u>Guru'Guay on La Cumparsita</u>[8]

MAY

12 San Pancracio Procession (Peregrinacion de San Pancracio), Parroquia Corazón de María, Centro. A religious festival in infamously secular Montevideo with a curious fair. On the **12th of every month** people visit the church to ask San Pancracio for work and good health. There are huge lines in general and also a street market.

18 Commemoration of the Battle of Las Piedras A public holiday

20 March of Silence (Marcha del Silencio) down 18 de Julio Avenue, demands the truth about the disappeared during the 1973-1986 dictatorship. 2016 is the 21st anniversary of the march.

JUNE

4* Tannat Wine and Lamb Festival (Festival del Tannat y el Cordero), associated vineyards in Montevideo and beyond

10 Afro-Uruguayan Heritage Day (Dia del Afrodescendiente) Afro-Uruguayans make up approx. 8% of the population

19 Commemoration of the birth of Artigas, liberator of Uruguay

23 Bonfires of San Juan (Hogueras de San Juan), Plaza Varela, Pocitos Midsummer celebrations

JULY

18 Constitution Day (Jura de la Constitución)

School holidays – two weeks packed with theatre and musical shows for children in Spanish

AUGUST

24 Nostalgia Night (Noche de la Nostalgia) A Golden Oldies celebration

25 Declaration of Independence

30 Santa Rosa Storm A storm which may (or may not) hit Montevideo five days before or after this

---

8   http://guruguay.com/worlds-most-famous-tango/

date, according to legend[9]

SEPTEMBER
8-19* Expo-PRADO, Prado Agricultural fair with gaucho competitions during the day and concerts every evening
8-14* Llamale H Gay film festival www.llamaleh.org
10-11* Heritage Day (Dia del Patrimonio) Historic buildings usually closed to the public open up over two days, street concerts, and more. Definitely worth checking out.
30 Diversity March (Marcha por la Diversidad) Montevideo's Pride celebrations (last Friday of September) See *Gay Montevideo*

OCTOBER
1-10* Montevideo Book Fair (Feria del Libro)
12 Columbus Day ("Día de la Raza" in Uruguay)
16-25* "Viva el Tango" Festival

NOVEMBER
2 All Souls Day
6* Festival de los Vinos Jovenes (Festival of Young Wines), associated vineyards

DECEMBER
3 Candombe Day (Dia del Candombe)
24 Christmas Eve celebrations, Port Market, Ciudad Vieja at midday
25 Christmas Day
31 New Year's Eve celebrations, Port Market, Ciudad Vieja at midday See Guru'Guay on Christmas and New Year in Montevideo[10]
31 New Year's Eve fireworks, Pocitos and Punta Carretas

Recommended festival and event website

I recommend that for a list of really wonderful events, check the Uruguayan Fiestas website[11]. It is in Spanish only but is a great resource, mainly visited by Uruguayans living in the interior. You will find umpteen gaucho rodeos and other unique events where you will likely be the only non-Uruguayan, but they will often only appear online a couple of weeks prior to the event. So check the site close to your time of arrival and see what you could have in store.

---

9   http://guruguay.com/climate-in-uruguay-annual-storm/
10 http://guruguay.com/montevideo-new-years-eve-christmas/
11 http://fiestasuruguayas.com.uy/

Where to stay in Montevideo

Montevideo is a small city of 1.5 million people and it's easy to get around. So really you could stay wherever you want, distance-wise.

However, Montevideo's neighbourhoods – or *barrios* – are all really different one from the other, and where you choose to stay can make a real difference to your time in Montevideo.

Here I cover the principal ones where most hotels are located and where as a visitor you are likely to want to stay. You'll notice that they are all strung along the 15-mile rambla (promenade) except for Centro.

The Guru's analysis of the best places to stay in Montevideo

Neighbourhoods

I want	Choose
Authentic Montevideo	Ciudad Vieja, Barrio Sur, Palermo
To be able to walk everywhere	Ciudad Vieja
The beach	Pocitos, Parque Rodo, Carrasco*
Great restaurants	Ciudad Vieja, Punta Carretas, Carrasco
Minimal cultural differences**	Punta Carretas, Carrasco
Closest to the airport	Carrasco

GURU'GUAY

* Beaches are accessible anywhere in Montevideo – Punta Carretas and Palermo (10-15 minutes walk), Ciudad Vieja, Barrio Sur and Centro (30-45 minutes walk along the rambla to Ramirez Beach in Parque Rodo or 5 minutes by taxi).

** Am I being flippant? Maybe.
Now let's have a look at the main selling points of each barrio.

Ciudad Vieja (the Old Town)

The Ciudad Vieja is Montevideo's historic centre and was once ALL of Montevideo. It is the heart of government, finance and import-export so it is bustling during the week and quieter on weekends. It is in a process of renovation and there are grandiose mansions next to pockets of poverty. This is no shiny for-export historic reconstruction – it is for real.

Thumbs up!
- ✔ You are in the heart of the historic area
- ✔ You can walk absolutely everywhere
- ✔ The Colonial Square and outstanding architecture
- ✔ Packed with historic cafes, theatres, live music, museums, galleries, auction-houses, antiques and old book stores
- ✔ The best restaurants in Montevideo, especially the lunch-time options
- ✔ Home to some of the most architecturally-charming hotels and accommodation.
- ✔ Right on the rambla, you can see the water at the end of every street – it's a peninsula with the River Plate on three sides
- ✔ The only really integrated neighbourhood where rich rub shoulders with poor
- ✔ Lively bar scenes on Bartolome Mitre and on the intersection of Ciudadela and Canelones

streets.

Mehhh

✗ May feel **deserted** on Saturday after 2 pm when most businesses close, Sundays and evenings – you need to have a plan (see "antidote" below).

✗ Good restaurants closed on Sundays, other than the Port Market.

✗ The area around the port like port areas all over the world – is dodgy after dusk. Simple solution: if you need to go there, take a cab, they are cheap.

Mehhh antidote

Plan to visit other neighbourhoods on **Sunday** for example

- Morning – check out the Tristan Narvaja flea market (20-minute walk)
- Sunday afternoon and evening – have lunch at the Port Market (weekends are the best days) or at the Bodega Bouza vineyard, have a siesta, then walk along the rambla, see the sun go down over the river and have dinner in Punta Carretas.

Plan to stay in the Ciudad Vieja on weekdays to see it at its bustling best (eg arrive Thursday midday and leave Sunday after lunch)

Punta Carretas

A smart upper-middle class residential barrio on the rambla.

Thumbs up!

✔ Close to the **rambla** for walking and running

✔ Lots of **restaurants**, cutesy tea-houses appearing

✔ Lots of **new hotels**

✔ 15-minute walk to Pocitos **Beach**

✔ Large shopping centre for those who need their **mall** fix.

Mehhh

- ✗ You will need to take transportation to sight-see
- ✗ The barrio's charming houses are being knocked down to make way for high-rises
- ✗ Not a great deal of character in the newer hotels, you could be anywhere really.

Pocitos

Pocitos is an upper-middle class neighbourhood close to the rambla dominated by high-rise apartments. It adjoins Punta Carretas.

Thumbs up!

- ✔ Has a very nice **beach** with fine white sand (by regular city beach standards – it's not Rio of course)
- ✔ Close to the **rambla**
- ✔ Lots of **restaurants**, cutesy tea houses, some craft beer spots
- ✔ Exploring further inland, old Pocitos has some charming labyrinth-like streets
- ✔ 15-20 minute walk to two malls.

Mehhh

- ✗ You will need to take transportation to sight-see
- ✗ The high-rises have removed a lot of the character.

Carrasco

The ritzy area of Montevideo which is primarily residential with low-level buildings and lots of greenery. It is closest to the airport on the rambla, which is dominated by the historic hotel pictured above. I've heard it joked that the children who grow up there are more familiar with Miami than they are with the centre of Montevideo.

Thumbs up!

- ✔ Has its own little **microcosm** with a main street, shops and restaurants
- ✔ **Sleek** hotels
- ✔ Has an extensive **beach**
- ✔ On the **rambla**
- ✔ All low-rise buildings with lots of green **leafy** streets
- ✔ Just 5-10 minutes drive from the **airport**.

Mehhh

- ✗ Far from "real Montevideo" and any of the sights
- ✗ Long cab ride to the city centre (we're talking approx. 30 USD one-way)
- ✗ The beach is not cleaned off-season and typically covered with washed-up debris between May and November.

Mehhh antidote

You can take a bus into the city centre, but if you are on a budget it does not make much sense to stay in Carrasco.

Centro = Holiday Inn

This is the downtown area dominated by the main avenue, 18 de Julio, which bustles day and night. On either side of the avenue there are lots of two and three star hotels.

Thumbs up!

- ✔ Bustling mid-week and on Saturday mornings
- ✔ Close to the Ciudad Vieja where many of the sights are
- ✔ Standard hotel accommodation tends to be **cheaper** here.

Mehhh

- ✗ The most urban part of Montevideo though still tree-lined with some trash issues
- ✗ 18 de Julio is not an attractive street until you look UP – and then there is the most amazing architecture
- ✗ Can be a little sketchy on side streets at night. Walk 18 de Julio to avoid problems or take the cheap cabs.

Parque Rodó, Palermo and Barrio Sur

There are not as many accommodation options in Parque Rodó, Barrio Sur or Palermo, the three areas located next to each other between Ciudad Vieja and Pocitos, so I'll group them together.

Thumbs up!

✔ **Charming neighbourhoods** filled with character and characters

✔ Mainly low-rise buildings on **leafy tree-lined streets**, though Palermo has seen a recent boom in high-rises

✔ Parque Rodó has the Playa Ramirez (Ramirez **beach**) - very shallow, it is ideal for small children

✔ Parque Rodó has two nostalgia-inspiring **parks** with fairgrounds for small children and overgrown!

✔ There's a **booming pub and bar scene** in Parque Rodó and several popular spots emerging at different points on Maldonado and Canelones streets.

✔ Barrio Sur is the heart of **Afro-Uruguayan culture**

✔ Drumming *comparsas* are out and about any night around 8pm in all three neighbourhoods throughout the year in preparation for Carnival.

Mehhh

✗ Most hotels are in the Barrio Sur neighbourhood which is a little sketchy, though improving. Take simple precautions to avoid problems.

✗ Pubs and bars tend to be spread-out and difficult to find. Make sure you have done your research and know where you are going to avoid disappointment.

Accommodation

Over the last few years, Montevideo has seen an explosion in hotel construction. We've gone from 60-plus hotels in 2010 to over 100. This means that there's currently a surplus of rooms and substantial reduction in prices which is great for customers. The bad news is that few of the hotels have anything unique about them; they could be anywhere in the world.

Montevideo has more art-deco buildings than any city in the world other than New York, so for this 2016 guide, I am going to highlight four hotels in different price brackets that are all architecturally lovely, as well as providing great service.

$$$$$ Sofitel Montevideo, Carrasco

Over my 15 years living in Montevideo I have watched the iconic art-deco building which dominates the rambla in Carrasco (pictured above) fall into disrepair, lie abandoned for years, take years to remodel, relaunch and start to function as a hotel before it was ready and get poor reviews, and now the Sofitel really seems to have found its place as a top five-star hotel with the most lavish decor you can imagine. The restaurant is also, according to local wine-expert colleagues, "faultless".

$$$$ Alma Historica Boutique Hotel, Ciudad Vieja

This year one of the best surprises for me as a small guesthouse owner has been to run into Caterina and Dario, a young Italian couple formerly based in London who fell in love with Montevideo just as my husband and I did and set up a lovely hotel in the Ciudad Vieja in support of an emblematic part of the city that other developers have shunned until very recently. The Alma Historica (which means Historic Soul) is located right on the edge of the lovely Plaza Zabala and has 12 rooms, each uniquely decorated, inspired by Uruguayan artists and creators. They are rightly at the top of the TripAdvisor Hotel ratings.

$$$ Casa Sarandi, Ciudad Vieja

Casa Sarandi is an award-winning art-deco guesthouse – the only inn in Montevideo in TripAdvisor's Top 5 Uruguayan B&Bs for two years running and top choice for the Lonely Planet – in Montevideo's Old City, surrounded by historic cafes, galleries, museums, bars, restaurants and the River Plate. Confession time. My husband Sergio and I run Casa Sarandi. In fact, Guru'Guay began on the insistence of my guests who were clamouring for decent information on Uruguay and insisted that we should turn our little guide for guests into something more complete, as the guidebooks were failing miserably. Our edge is providing you with insider info that will make your stay in Montevideo unforgettable. Thousands of people visit Guru'Guay each month but when you stay with us you get the inside scoop personally – even before you arrive if that's what you need. Our rooms are all individually decorated with private bathroom, queen-size beds and imported linen.

$$ Hotel Palacio, Ciudad Vieja

I stayed in the Hotel Palacio the first time I ever came to Montevideo when I lived in Buenos Aires in the 1990s. It was a charming vintage budget hotel. Vintage in the sense that nothing had been updated in decades – and things have not changed! This is very much a slightly tired two-star hotel with rooms for less than 50 USD but packed with character. They have won the TripAdvisor Travellers Choice Award several years running in the budget category. The Palacio is run by a very friendly family – Fernando answers mails, his mum Rosa is on the desk. Fernando's English is great. The desk staff's English is non-existent but you will get by. There's a classic wrought-iron elevator, marble staircases and the rooms on the sixth floor have balconies.

Personal safety

Montevideo is one of the safest cities in Latin America but it is still a capital city and an unlucky traveller could encounter small-scale crime.

One thing that may surprise you is that Montevideans will look out for you, sometimes literally stopping you in the street and telling you to be careful. This tends to worry travellers initially, but once you have spent a few days in Montevideo you'll realise that, especially if you are a seasoned traveller, you can take this advice with a pinch of salt.

Take the regular precautions that you would when you are in a capital city and you should be just fine. That advice goes for any neighbourhood, the upscale ones too.

Tips for staying safe

- **Don't carry your passport** No one will ask you for it (or a photocopy will be fine).
- You'll be more comfortable if you **blend in**. Don't walk around flashing money, expensive equipment or talking at the top of your voice in English.
- **Feel confident about stopping a taxi in the street** – they are very secure and cheap. It's normal to ask your restaurant hosts to call you a cab at the end of the evening.
- Going out at night, **if you don't need to carry a bag, don't carry one** – put the money you need and a credit card in your pocket and voilà!
- **Keep a 20-peso bill separate in your pocket** in case you decide to respond to a panhandler.
- **Avoid withdrawing money from ATMs after dark** and from those on the street.
- **Stick to well-lit areas** at night.
- **Don't leave anything of value in view in a hire car**. Even a jacket might be a temptation in an unattended car.
- **Don't feel nervous** when Montevideans insist on telling you to be take care when you are on the street. They are just looking out for you.

Tips for specific neighbourhoods

- **Ciudad Vieja** The area around the port is dodgy after dark – like port areas all over the world. If visiting the port area at night, take a cab. The area near the Teatro Solis sees regular movement at night and you can feel comfortable walking and taking the bus.
- **Centro** When walking in the Centro area after dark, stick to the main avenue 18 de Julio and then cut down to your destination, rather than taking quieter side streets.

- **El Cerro** This is not an ideal district for strolling, though it has the best view of the Bay of Montevideo. If you visit the fort across the bay, you may want to go by taxi and have the driver wait for you.
- **Mercado del Puerto** at the weekend and the **Tristan Narvaja street market** on Sundays Beware of pickpockets and confidence tricksters running card games particularly at the busiest periods such as during December.

Improvements to safety in the Ciudad Vieja

At the end of 2013 the Montevideo government cracked down on street crime in the centre of Montevideo and the Old City. The muggings were being carried out by a handful of adults and children who had become increasingly brazen.

Unfortunately because this small gang targeted the Old City, an unmissable stop on any traveller's itinerary, a lot got written online when really the overall level of crime did not warrant the focus of attention. Fortunately, since the installation of the cameras, the situation is much improved.

So take the regular precautions you should in any capital city and you should be fine. Enjoy!

Finding your way around

Montevideo is a relatively small city and easy to get around on foot or by bus.

To give you an idea, you can easily walk along the rambla from the Old City to Montevideo's oldest park, Parque Rodó in just 45-50 minutes. I find that most of my guests tend to walk places and then catch a bus back to the guesthouse.

Maps

When you arrive in Montevideo, chances are your hotel will provide you with a very useful map produced by the Montevideo Government tourism office.

The map covers all the areas that you are likely to visit and so there is no need to bring another map, unless you are an enthusiast.

You can also pick up this map at any tourist information centre or in the lobby of some of the bigger hotels. You will recognise it because it does not have any advertising on it.

Website recommendation: Como Ir

Como Ir[12] is a beautifully designed, fast website which shows you how to get anywhere in Montevideo on foot or by bus.

You'll need to read some Spanish but really very basic. I recommend checking out the site video demo, even if you don't speak Spanish, as it shows you visually how to use the site (note, this demo was not working at the time of finalising this guide). For instance you'll see that you must type the first letters of the address and then wait for the text predictor to show you street options to select from.

How to use the Como Ir website

1. Under **origen y destino** (starting point and end point), open the first drop-down box (**tipo de ubicación** i.e type of place). Choose from:

- **Esquina o dirección** – to search by street name and number (*dirección*) or cross streets (*esquina*), type in the street name under *calle*, and the cross street under *esquina/numero*
- **Lugar de interés** – place of interest, under which you can sub-search place types (*tipo de lugar*) like:
  - **Cultura** place of cultural interest
  - **Deporte** sports venue
  - **Espacio libre** open air venue e.g. a park
  - **Monumento** monument
  - **Playa** beach
- **Calle** – street, if you just have the street name and not street name and number of your destination, or to find where a street is located
- **Linea de omnibus** – bus line, handy if the 32 bus, for example, passes your hotel door and you'd like to see where it would take you.

2. Click on **marcar origen** to mark your starting point and **marcar destino** to choose your end point or destination. You can also drag the start and end pins onto your map if it's easier that way.

3. Click **ir en ómnibus** to be shown the bus routes. Click on the bus options in **resultados** to see the bus routes appear on the map. Click **ir caminando** to be shown a route to walk.

4. To see schedules click on **horarios**.

Como Ir also has a mobile app. Though it does less than the website – for instance you must have street numbers or cross streets to hand – and it's not so easy to compare the directness of bus routes, it is handy to be able to follow a map on your phone.

Como Ir is created by the Montevideo city government.

---

12 http://comoir.montevideo.gub.uy/

Using public transport

Montevideo has a very good public transport system and you should feel confident about using it.

Local buses

Everyone uses buses. A ticket costs less than a dollar and services are frequent.

To **stop the bus**, wait at the bus stop and then extend your arm to indicate for it to stop. On the bus you pay the driver or sometimes there is a conductor sitting slightly further back on the left.

The **standard ticket** is called a *común*. At the time of writing it cost 26 pesos. You do not need to have exact change, though obviously coins and smaller notes are preferred.

There is a *céntrico* bus which constantly goes up and down the principal downtown avenue 18 de Julio from the main Tres Cruces bus station to the Plaza de Independencia. This bus costs 19 pesos.

Long distance buses

You can take **buses all over Uruguay and even to other countries** in South America from the **Tres Cruces bus station**. The good news is that buses tend to be very frequent. Unless you are buying at very short notice in days of highest demand, you should not have a problem getting tickets.

Bus timetables are online at www.trescruces.com.uy. The website is in Spanish only so if you need help you can find out how to read the timetables on the Guru'Guay website.

Off season you can **book seats by phone** and pick up and pay for the tickets not later than 30 minutes before the bus departs.

It's now possible to **buy tickets online** with a number of companies using a credit card. The sites that I have checked (e.g. COT and TURIL, both of which go to Colonia) are in **Spanish only**. So make sure you turn on your online translator or have a dictionary handy.

Alternatively try **giving the companies a call** (numbers are on the website mentioned above). I managed to talk to a very friendly English-speaking agent when I called last week and was able to buy my guest's ticket over the phone giving credit card and passport details.

Taxis

Feel comfortable flagging a taxi in the street or calling by phone. They are reasonably cheap and safe. You'll know if a taxi is free because it has a red light in the front windscreen.

Usually taxi drivers are very civilised. The worst a driver could do, noticing you are from out of town, is *"pasear"* i.e. take the long way round. If you want to avoid this, BEFORE you get in the cab hand over the address you are going to on paper and ask how much it will cost (*"Cuanto puede salir?"*). Drivers can contact their HQ to check the price. If the driver is not prepared to do this, just say *"Muchas gracias"* and walk away.

Giving an address Uruguayans give directions by referring to **the street and the cross street**. So for example, to go to Bluzz Bar which is on Florida street close to the corner of Canelones street, you would tell the taxi driver to take you to "Florida *esquina* Canelones". Or of course you could just give the street address and number! **I've actually provided a number of addresses in this way using "esquina" throughout the guide.** You pronounce it *es-KEEN-ah*.

Metres All taxis in Montevideo are **metred**. But what shows up on the screen is NOT usually what you pay, though some metres show prices too. Usually the metre number (called *"fichas"*) is not the same as the price. At the end of your trip, the driver will consult a laminated chart hanging in the cab and look up the number of *fichas*. There will be a corresponding amount in pesos – that is the cost of your ride. There is one chart for travel during the daytime and a table for nighttime and public holidays on the back.

Have change If you are going a short distance, avoid paying with bills over 200 pesos.

If you only have a 1000 peso bill, BEFORE you get into the cab ask the driver if s/he has change (*"Tengo mil pesos. Tenés cambio?"*). Avoid this problem at the ATM by withdraw an amount that will give you change, e.g. 3900 pesos, rather than 4000.

Tipping Uruguayans do not tip taxi drivers. Even for longer drives, e.g. to the airport, a tip is optional. See *Tipping*

Luggage Open the front passenger door and put your luggage on the seat next to the driver. Only if your luggage is really bulky will the driver (finally) descend and open the trunk for you. Don't expect him to load the luggage for you there, either.

Times when it may be hard to get a taxi

It's usually easy to get hold of a taxi except for:

- Changes of shifts (around 3-4 pm in the afternoon)
- Rainy days
- After 4 pm on Christmas Eve
- After 4 pm on New Years Eve. Don't expect to get a cab on January 1 until 4 am at the earliest.

Sample taxi charges

At the time of writing rough estimates are:

- The port to Centro – roughly 80 pesos (approx. 3 USD)
- Ciudad Vieja to Tres Cruces bus station or Punta Carretas – roughly 170 pesos (approx. 6 USD)
- Ciudad Vieja to Bouza Vineyard (13.5 km) – roughly 450 pesos (approx. 15 USD)

Calling a cab when you don't speak Spanish – in Montevideo it's simple

Of course now there are lots of phone apps that you can use but I believe in supporting local initiatives. Montevideo taxi company Radiotaxi has an automated service which will get a taxi to you in just THREE minutes and you don't even have to speak with anyone. Ah, Montevideo is just so darn civilised. Here's what to do:

- Dial 141.
- An automated voice starts, press 1. The system will look for the nearest taxi.
- Then you will be told *"El movil numero xxx pasará por usted en 3 minutos"*. That is: "Car number xxx will pick you up in 3 minutes". It is never more nor less.
- Put the phone down and go outside to wait for your cab. The taxi will arrive with zero pesos on the clock.

If you do speak Spanish and would like to speak to a human being, the other big taxi company does not use an automated system. You can call them at 1771.

Oh and of course there are always internet apps that you can use like VoyEnTaxi (and controversially at the time of writing, Uber).

Driving and car rental

Driving in Montevideo is fairly easy and driving outside of Montevideo is a doodle as the roads are mainly empty other than on holiday weekends.

Is it worth hiring a car while in Montevideo? I don't think so, unless you are staying in Carrasco or some other far-flung barrio. Distances are short, public transport is great and taxis cheap. Only vineyards are further afield, and Uruguay has a zero-tolerance drunk-driving policy.

Tips for when you are leaving the city in your hire-car

- Avoid driving in the congested city centre. It's far easier to **stick to the rambla** and then cut up to your destination when you are close. MUCH less stressful.
- You must **turn on your low-beam headlights at all times** during the day. It's obligatory anywhere in Uruguay including cities.
- There are just a few **rush hours** – around 8.30-9 am going in to Montevideo and 4-7 pm leaving. There are just a few bottlenecks on the rambla but if you want to avoid congestion, then avoid these times.
- When to **give way** to oncoming cars when there's no "Alto" sign? Locals will tell you you should give way to cars coming on your right, but it's not that clearcut in Montevideo. The best I can explain is that if you are driving parallel to the rambla, in general you have right of way, except in a very few cases. Of course this means knowing where you are and that is not easy to know if you are new to the city. This is another reason to always take the rambla as far to your destination as you can!

Car hire

The international car rental companies are all present in Montevideo along with a number of local companies. It appears you get best rates if you book before arriving.

Deductible If you do not take out full insurance at the time you hire your car, you will be asked to sign a credit card voucher called a "deductible", which is "deducible" in Spanish (you say it ded-oo-SEE-blay). The value of the voucher is typically 1000 USD for a compact car (more for a larger car). This means that the insurance covers you for everything except the first 1000 USD worth of damage. This is standard practice for Uruguayan car rentals. The voucher will be ripped up at the end of your rental.

VAT–off car rental

To encourage tourism, the Uruguayan government is currently eliminating the 22% VAT from car hire. The offer applies to all non-Uruguayan credit and debit cards. With VISA, the discount appears automatically on your bill. With MasterCard you will see the deduction on your monthly statement.

Recommended car hire company

I get asked all the time about reliable car hire in Uruguay so I'll give a shout-out to a local company, Mariño Sport[13], which has offices in Montevideo, Colonia and Punta del Este. I have been recommending them to our guesthouse clients and my own visiting friends and family since 2010 and I have been consistently impressed by their great service and personal touch.

---

13 http://www.mariniosport.com/

Back a few years ago, I had a French guest whose rental car window got broken by an opportunistic thief. She was pretty upset – not only because of the unwelcome complication but she was naturally worried about the repair charges. Not only did Mariño come to sort out the damage immediately but they did not even charge her! How many big companies would take that attitude?

Free drop-off and pick-up wherever you request This is really a great part of the service. You can arrange to have them meet you at the airport, the port or your hotel and then they will pick the car up from you wherever you decide in Montevideo. It can also save you money too as a taxi from the airport to the centre of Montevideo can set you back over 30 USD. You can also drop-off in Colonia or Punta del Este for an additional fee.

No hidden extras The rate they quote you will include:
- All taxes
- Full insurance
- A designated second driver for free
- 350 kilometre per day limit (e.g. Punta del Este is 132 km from Montevideo)
- Full 24-hour mechanical assistance throughout Uruguay.

My clients who've gone with cheaper companies have been messed around regarding how much gas was in the car to start with and other such annoying tricks.

10% off with Guru'guay You can email car-rental@guruguay.com quoting offer code Guru'Guay for a 10% discount. Write "Guru'Guay car rental: your name " in your subject line. A word of warning: Don't be put off by their terrible written English, you will work things out.

Tipping

Tipping in Montevideo is fairly straightforward. It tends to be voluntary, and so much appreciated.

Restaurants & cafes

Unless service has been particularly poor I would recommend tipping **10%** of your bill. If you order just a drink, rounding up your change to the nearest 10 is fine.

In general restaurants **do not charge a service charge**. I think I have only ever seen it included on a bill in the Port Market in one of the more touristy venues.

Taxis

Uruguayans do not tip taxi drivers. Even on longer drives, for example from the centre of Montevideo to the airport, a tip is optional. Really, it is perfectly acceptable to sit there and wait for your 5 pesos change if you wish.

As a consequence, do not expect your driver to do *anything* to help you unless specifically asked. If you particularly liked the driver, tip up to 10%. Rounding-up is also appreciated as they are usually strapped for change.

Baggage handlers & hotel porters

At the **airport**, tip the handler **20 pesos** (a dollar bill is always handy tip material in Latin America). Same goes for a hotel porter. If you want to **avoid handlers** at the airport look steelily ahead as they approach you and do not engage in conversation.

Using the **long-distance bus** system, if your bag goes into the hold, you might tip the baggage handler a few coins (though fewer people do this in Uruguay than I notice they do in Argentina).

Street parking attendants

Informal parking attendants or *cuidacoches* have been a feature of Montevideo since the 1930s. They guide you into your parking space on the street. They are supposed to watch over your car while you are away, though how they are going to alert you if there's a problem escapes me.

Cuidacoches should be government-registered however you are under no obligation whatsoever to tip. According to studies, *cuidacoches* are typically in their late 40s, have completed primary school and have fallen on hard times. Most consider themselves part of the local scenery and carry out their role with good humour. Which means that most residents of Montevideo tip them.

When you return to your car, tip **10 pesos**. If you have just parked for just a few minutes **a couple of coins** is fine. **At night**, tip more generously, such as a **20-peso note**.

If you don't have change, this apology – *"Disculpe, te voy a tener que deber"* (Sorry, I'll have to owe you) – will elicit a good-natured thumbs-up and "No problem, neighbour!" response. And if it doesn't – well, we all have bad days.

Petrol station attendants

No petrol station in Uruguay is self-service. As well as pump petrol, attendants will wash your windscreen, fill your windscreen wiper bottle and put air in your tyres on request. A 10-peso tip is appreciated for any service beyond pumping gas.

Windscreen cleaners

These guys jump out at traffic lights and offer to clean your front or back windows. If you accept, give them a few coins, say 5 pesos. If you don't want or need your screen cleaned, just shake your head, say no, and look straight ahead. Don't make eye contact! If you do, before you know it, they'll be squirting soapy water all over your windshield.

Wi–Fi, internet connectivity and phones

One of the great things about travelling in Uruguay is that free Wi-Fi is available everywhere. Hotels provide it for free. Restaurants and cafes too. The airport Wi-Fi is free. Long distance buses have free internet connections.

Even local buses have Wi-Fi! Check out your Wi-Fi connections on any Montevideo street and see bus companies CUTCSA and COT with their respective bus numbers appearing and then disappearing on your network list.

Uruguay is the first country in the world to completely implement the One Laptop Per Child initiative. Every child in the public education system in both primary and secondary school has an XO laptop. The project began in the interior of the country (reversing the typical tendency for the capital city, where half of Uruguay's population lives, to get new developments first) and only rolled out in the capital once the entire of the interior was covered. Wi-Fi connections are broadcast from school buildings, so it's typical to see small children with their XOs perched in plazas or school steps out of school time.

Disappointingly, going against this positive trend, Buquebus, the international ferry company, charges for connectivity on their Argentina-Uruguay crossings. So check your email at the port before you leave.

Getting a Uruguayan SIM card for your mobile phone

Go to any shopping centre and pick up a chip there. They cost 200 pesos and you get credit on your phone immediately. You can buy them anonymously.

The companies available are ANTEL, Claro and Movistar. If you want to support the local telecoms company, which provides really good on-site technical support, use ANTEL.

Getting internet on your phone

Warning: You will need to replace your SIM card with a Uruguayan one. But if you are fine about doing that, then this is a very cheap way to enable your smart-phone.

- Buy an ANTEL phone chip at a shopping centre or phone shop. The most convenient will be the Punta Carretas Shopping Centre because technical assistance is right next door
- Take your phone and new chip to the nearest ANTEL office; there is one next to Punta Carretas Shopping Centre as well as an office in the city centre.
- Go to the information desk and ask for a technician to configure your chip for internet. Say *"Me pueden configurar internet?"* (meh pweh-den con-feeg-oo-rar internet).You will be directed to take a number for the technical staff and will need to wait till your number comes up.
- Once your chip has been configured you need to send an SMS to ANTEL to request internet megabytes for your phone. Send the SMS to the number 226. In your message put the number of pesos' worth of internet bandwidth credit you would like, e.g. "100". You can charge anything from 50 pesos and up. For those staying a while, note that 100 pesos lasts for up to one month depending on your use, 200 pesos for two months. With 100 pesos I find that I can do everything that I want to on my smart-phone for a month. I have never run out of credit except for when I used WhatsApp talk intensively for a few hours.
- If you'd like to check your credit, send the word *"Saldo"* in an SMS to the same number.

ANTEL offices with technical support Only two ANTEL offices offer technical assistance – the ANTEL office right next to Punta Carretas Shopping Centre on Garcia Cortina street (almost on the corner of Ellauri) or the ANTEL office on the corner of San Jose and Paraguay streets in Centro.

Opening times The ANTEL offices open Monday-Friday 9 am-7 pm and Saturdays 9 am-2 pm and they can get very busy. The best time to go is between 9 am and 10 am.

Calling Uruguay

The international Uruguay country code is **+598**.

Is the number I need to call a cell phone? All Uruguayan mobile phone numbers begin with 09. To call one from an international phone use the country code and drop the 0. So to call 099 606058, call +598 99 606058.

The number I need to call has seven digits and does not work

The Uruguay phone numbering system was updated from 7 to 8 digits a number of years ago. If the number you need to call uses the old system, don't worry, it's easy to fix. For numbers in Montevideo add a 2 in front, and add a 4 for numbers in the rest of Uruguay. So if the number you need to call is 500 4567 and it's in Montevideo, change it to 2500 4567.

Exchanging money

Exchanging cash is cheap and easy. You can change money in an exchange bureau (cambio) or a bank. Some people experience problems withdrawing from ATMs including low limits.

- You do not need to show ID.
- You won't be charged a commission.
- The best exchange rate is given for US dollars with Euros a close second. There is very little difference between buying and selling US dollars.

Generally exchange bureaus (except for the thieving hounds at the airport) offer similar rates. I have noticed that the exchanges in some of the posher neighbourhoods like Carrasco and Pocitos maybe very slightly less competitive than in the city centre.

If you are exchanging more than 100 dollars ask the teller what their best rate is (say, "*Cual es tu mejor cambio para 200 USD?*"). You will invariably get approx. 0.25 pesos more for your dollar, which can mount up.

No commission charged

Take advantage of this. If you have excess Brazilian reals or Argentinian pesos, it might well be worth your while changing them into dollars before you move on, given you don't have to pay commission.

If you exchange too many pesos, it is worth changing your excess back into USD before you move on to your next destination.

Do not buy pesos at home or at the airport

Wait until you get to Uruguay to exchange your money. All my guests who have tried getting hold of pesos before they travel have gotten very bad rates - IF they have been able to get hold of pesos at all.

The airport also has very bad rates (paying out 20% less on average).

If you need money straight away, withdraw money at one of the airport ATMs and plan to exchange in the city centre.

Bank and exchange opening and closing times

Money exchanges in Montevideo are open regular business hours, typically **9 am till 7 pm Monday to Friday** and **Saturdays 9am-1pm**. You can find money exchanges all over the city. Look out for the "cambio" sign.

To exchange on **weekends** or until 10 pm, go to a shopping mall.

Banks open Monday to Friday from **1pm to 5pm**. Yes, they are closed in the mornings.

Withdrawing cash at ATMs

ATMs dispense Uruguayan pesos – and US dollars! There are ATMs in the airports, bus stations and at the port in Montevideo. Uruguay has **two ATM networks – Red BROU** and **Banred**. If one does not work for you, try the other.

Use the **terminals** that have Cirrus/Maestro/Link/VISA and other stickers on them. The other terminals are for Uruguayan card users only.

ATM withdrawal limits and charges

Some visitors complain that they can only withdraw a small amount of cash from ATMs in Uruguay.

At the time of writing, **Banred** has a **300 USD limit** or 5000 pesos at one time. As 300 USD will currently buy you almost 9000 pesos, go for dollars and then exchange. **RedBROU** has a limit of just **200 USD** and 5000 pesos. So **use Banred**.

The **withdrawal fees** in Uruguay vary but you can expect to pay between 3-6 USD per withdrawal to the Uruguayan bank, as well as your own bank fees.

Having problems withdrawing from ATMs?

I called the Banred network to find out a number of **ATMs that should work with international cards**.

Time of day For some weird reason as an international card holder you may only be able to **withdraw from 11am to 7pm**. So do keep this in mind.

Recommended ATMs They also provided me with a short list of some centrally-located ATMs that should work with your international card if you are having problems:

Ciudad Vieja
Sarandi 402 on the corner of Zavala (Bandes Bank)
Zavala 1463 on the corner of 25 de mayo (Itau)
Centro
18 de Julio and Julio Herrera (Santander)
18 de Julio and Paraguay (Bandes)
18 de Julio and Ejido (Itau)
Tres Cruces and Punta Carretas shopping malls (not the Montevideo mall)

More reading on Guru'Guay.com
This information is up-to-date of January 2016. To get the latest information on money and potential problems, check out my article on withdrawing money from ATMs[14] to see if there are any updates (make sure you check out the comments too)

Do Uruguayan businesses accept dollars or Argentine pesos?

It is best to pay with Uruguayan pesos; however, many businesses or even taxis are likely to accept smaller dollar bills if you are in a tight spot.

Cashing cheques and travelers cheques

Don't bring travelers cheques. It's only possible to exchange them in a very few specific banks, and then a substantial commission is charged.

One Guru'Guay reader wrote: "It was very hard to find an office who changed me AmericanExpress

---

14 http://guruguay.com/atm-problems-uruguay/

Travel checks to USD! The official charge is 2% and one requested an additional of 12%, which means a change loss of 14%. A rip off! Finally Delta Services Rio Negro 1341 (close to the rip off) did it for totally of 4%."

As would happen in almost any country, don't expect to be able to cash a regular check from your bank in Uruguay.

Why do I see the price in dollars everywhere?

In Uruguay, $ is the symbol for… pesos!

The symbol Uruguayans use for US dollars is U$S or US$ or USD.

However, Uruguayans, like the citizens of many other Latin American nations, typically save in dollars. So don't be surprised to see property prices, rental values and the price of electrical and luxury goods labelled in dollars.

Credit card VAT refunds

The Uruguayan government offers a great benefit to tourists. When you use a foreign credit card in Uruguay you get the 22% VAT deducted from restaurant bills and car hire – obviously saving you a huge amount.

The VAT discounts apply to restaurants and car hire (hotel rooms are already tax free).

The full list of VAT deductions includes:
- Self-drive car or vehicle hire
- Hospitality services at restaurants, bars, pubs, cafes, hotels and hostels, except for the cost of accommodation
- Catering and other services for parties and events.

This offer applies to all non-Uruguayan credit and debit cards.

The most popular credit cards in Uruguay are VISA (by far – 70% of the market), followed by MasterCard and the local OCA card. American Express and Diners are rarely accepted.

With VISA, the discount appears automatically on your bill. With MasterCard you will see the deduction on your monthly statement.

At the time of writing, the rebate is offered until March 31, 2016. However, it has been extended multiple times in the last few years, and I can see no reason why in March 2016 it will not be extended again.

VAT in Spanish is called "IVA" (pronounced *EE-vah*).

More reading on Guru'Guay.com
I'll keep this article "Use your credit card and get 22% VAT off"[15] updated with the latest information so that you can find out if the legislation is renewed throughout 2016.

---

15 http://guruguay.com/use-credit-card-get-vat-off/

THINGS
TO DO

Things To Do

10 architectural delights

The beginning of the 1900s in Uruguay was a period of extraordinary change and progress, which was reflected in the 1930s by a golden era in architecture. Architects like Julio Vilamajó and Mauricio Cravotto were at the vanguard – designing modernist houses and buildings in the very heart of the city – when state-of-the-art buildings by European contemporaries like Le Corbusier were exiled to areas far away from city centres.

There are hundreds of wonderful buildings to see in Montevideo. For this selection, I have focused on places where you can actually go and wander round. But when you are on the streets, do look out for buildings, including many homes "signed" by architectural giants like Vilamajó, Cravotto and Scasso.

Palacio Taranco, Plaza Zabala, Ciudad Vieja

Now housing the Museum of Decorative Arts, the Taranco Palace was originally a family home built in 1908. It was inspired by 18th century French architecture and the construction materials and furniture were imported from Paris.

Jockey Club, 18 de Julio 857, Centro

Stunning social club built in 1920 with a restaurant which opens for lunch and dinner. It's a national heritage site, pictured above.

Clube Brasileiro, 18 de Julio 994, Centro

Located on the second floor (take the fabulous wrought-iron elevator), you can visit the restaurant which has high stained-glass windows and art-deco mosaic floors. Opens Mon-Sat 8 am-9 pm. Also see *Breakfast*

Palacio Legislativo, at the end of Rondeau Avenue, Aguada

The seat of the Uruguayan government, the Palace was built on land donated in 1866. The building is in an eclectic style and was inaugurated in 1925. It has an enormous salon known as the Lost Footsteps Salon as you cannot hear footsteps. Wonderful murals. There is a great little tour in English at 10.30 am and 3 pm which starts at the back entrance and costs just 70 pesos. The area was traditionally where fruit and vegetables from the countryside arrived in Montevideo for sale. The Montevideo Agricultural Market is close by. Also see *Tours*

Montevideo Agricultural Market (Mercado Agricola de Montevideo, or MAM), José L. Terra 2220, Aguada

An impressive iron-work structure. You can see something similar in the Mercado del Puerto. Built close by the Legislative Palace, the market was the initiative of five private individuals who donated their land in 1903 with the premise that the market would be state-of-the-art. The market began functioning in 1912. It fell into abandon by the end of the century. It was reopened in 2013 as a shopping centre with a couple of good restaurants. Open every day 8 am-10 pm. Combine with a visit to the Palacio Legislativo and Parque El Prado or Montevideo's Contemporary Arts Space.

Hotel del Prado, Gabriela Mistral 4223, Prado

Built in 1912 as a recreation centre in the centre of the lovely Prado Park, the building fell into disuse by the 1950s and it was only recently that the building has been recovered and turned into an elegant hotel and tea-room. Combine this with a visit to the Museo Blanes, Prado Park and botanical gardens.

Montevideo Yacht Club, Port of Buceo

This nautical-style tower pictured below built in the 1930s and shaped like a ship stands over the marina. After a walk around the marina and along the waterfront, have a bite to eat in El Italiano, the open-air restaurant close by.

Casa Zorrilla de San Martin, José Luis Zorrilla De San Martín 96, Punta Carretas

A testimony to what the family homes of Punta Carretas and Pocitos all looked like in the 1900s when they were first built. This house was designed by its owner, the artist Juan Zorrilla de San Martin, and is now a museum. Open Mon-Sat 1-6 pm.

Peñarol Railway Industrial Heritage Centre (Centro de barrio del Peñarol), Sayago 1584 esq Av Aparicio Saravia, Peñarol

A far-flung working class neighbourhood was the centre of Montevideo's rail industry run by the British from 1891 until it fell into abandonment. A regeneration movement has converted the old railway station into an industrial museum and Uruguay has presented this neighbourhood centre for recognition as a UNESCO heritage site. The railway station master's house and the railworkers' cottages were built by British railway workers and are of a style that only exists in one village in the UK nowadays, and on the streets of iconic Fray Bentos in Western Uruguay.

Recommended Architectural and Urban Guide to Montevideo

To get your architectural juices flowing, check out the **Architectural and Urban Guide to Montevideo** – a little gem I unearthed on the local government website. In English and Spanish, the guide is beautifully designed and perfect for curious travellers and photographers. It includes almost 400 buildings and spaces organised by neighbourhood.
See <u>Guru'Guay for more info and to download</u>[16]

---

16 http://guruguay.com/montevideo-architecture-guide/

Museums

Most of Montevideo's museums are free to the public. It is a real shame that most museums don't include any information in English and that they do not tend to open on weekends. Fortunately art museums (in the next chapter) are open on weekends.

The best explanation that I've been volunteered for why this is, is that the local government appears to envisage the majority of visitors to museums as being local schoolchildren.

Andes 1972 Museum

Rincón 619, Ciudad Vieja

The story of the Andes plane crash survivors (all Uruguayans) is one of the great human survival stories of the 20th century[17] and it is beautifully told here and will move you. The museum website recommends the visit for adults and children over 12, and that if you plan to take younger children, you should talk to them first about what they are going to hear. This is good advice. This story is not for the faint-hearted. Exhibit in English, Spanish and German with tours in the three languages. Entrance fee is a well-deserved 200 pesos for this invaluable privately run initiative. If you go to just one museum while you are in Montevideo, make it this one.

Mon-Fri 10-5 pm, Sat 10-3 pm

---

17 http://guruguay.com/andes-1972-museum/

Carnival Museum (Museo del Carnaval)

Rambla 25 de Agosto de 1825 Nr. 218, Ciudad Vieja

The Uruguayan Carnival is one of the best-kept secrets in South America! The carnival competition lasts more than 40 days starting at the end of January and ending in mid-March and is said to be the longest Carnival competition in the world. Uruguayan Carnival fanatics compete in five different categories and at the Carnival Museum you will be given an insight into the two most popular carnival categories – *candombe* and *murga*. The exhibitions are backed with interactive technology, videos and music. The museum is right next to the Mercado del Puerto. The entrance fee is 100 pesos per person. Children under 12 enter for free.

December-March: Daily 11 am-5 pm, April-November: Wed-Sun 11-5 pm

Decorative Arts Museum (Museo de Artes Decorativos)

25 de Mayo 376, just off Plaza Zabala, Ciudad Vieja

Also known as the Palacio Taranco, the house was designed by the architect of the Arc de Triomphe for a wealthy merchant who imported all his fixtures and fittings from Europe. Built in 1908 on the site of Montevideo's first theatre, the house is packed full of hand-painted grand pianos, Flemish tapestries and a life-sized marble flamenco dancer in the hallway. There is almost no signage but it is still great to see how the other half lived over a hundred years ago in Montevideo.

Mon-Fri 12.30 am-5.40 pm

Gaucho Museum and the Mint Museum

18 de Julio 998, Centro

The extravagant French and Italian-style "palace" built in 1896 housing these two museums is reason alone to visit. The Gaucho Museum, pictured at the top of the page, hosts a stunning collection of horse gear, silver and gold spurs, ornate belts, mate gourds (used for the ritual drink in this part of the world) and tobacco-smoking gear, many more than 150 years old. The sword of revolutionary Aparicio Saravia is amongst the beautifully crafted swords and daggers. For Uruguayan supporters of the National political party, this is like stumbling upon Excalibur! The Mint Museum hosts artifacts from the National Bank including counting machines and enormous hand-written ledgers which will send shivers down the spine of any accountant. Combine with a visit to Clube Brasileiro for a bite to eat (see *Historic cafes*).

Mon-Fri 10-4 pm

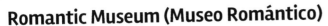

Romantic Museum (Museo Romántico)

25 de Mayo 434, Ciudad Vieja
A few steps away from Plaza Zabala, the building that houses the Romantic Museum was built in 1831 by a businessman and was considered one of the most luxurious residences at the time of Uruguayan independence. It was sometimes called the "Marble Palace" because there was so much marble ornamentation. In 1962 it became the Romantic Museum, depicting the social and economic conditions of Montevideo's upper classes from the 1830s to 1900. It has a lovely, serene patio and furniture and is a pleasant place to sit in peace for a little while.
Wed-Sun 11-4.45 pm

National Football Museum (Museo del Futbol)

Parque Centenario (entrance on the east side of the stadium)

Peñarol Football Club Museum (Museo del Club Atlético Peñarol)

Cerro Largo esq. Magallanes, Centro
Uruguay hosted the first ever World Cup in 1930 and La Celeste, as Uruguay's national soccer team is known, has won more international football cup titles than any other in the world. Not bad for a country of just three million. There are two football museums in Montevideo – the National Football Museum in the Centenario Stadium where the first World Cup was won, and the Peñarol Museum in celebration of the achievements of Uruguay's most popular football team. Both are enjoyable to visit, even for non-football fans like myself. However, the lack of English signage makes a guided tour with the Futbol Fanáticos a great idea.
National Football Museum Mon-Fri 10-5 pm
Peñarol Football Club Museum Fri 1-5 pm, Sat 11-6 pm, Sun 11-3 pm (closed all January) See *Tours*

Art galleries and museums

Montevideo has a bunch of public art museums. There are very few private galleries with exhibitions; instead most galleries are primarily dedicated to selling. Most art museums are free of charge to enter and unlike regular museums tend to be open on weekends. Private museums charge a small fee.

Art museums

National Museum of Visual Arts (Museo Nacional de Artes Visuales)

Julio Herrera y Reissig esq. Tomás Giribaldi, Parque Rodó
Uruguay's most important art museum, its collection has more than 6,000 pieces by national artists including the most well-known Uruguayan painters – Juan Manuel Blanes , Carlos Federico Sáez, Pedro Figari, Rafael Barradas and Joaquín Torres García. The limited space means that only a small percentage are on display. The temporary exhibits include Uruguayan and international artists. Combine with a visit to the Playa Ramirez beach.
Tues-Sun 2-7 pm

Museo Blanes

Av Millán 4015, El Prado
Uruguayan art ranging from the nation's founding to the present day including Figari and Blanes of

course. A picture by Blanes is featured at the top of this page. There is also a Japanese Garden in the lovely mansion in the leafy Prado neighbourhood that houses the museum. Combine this with a visit to the Botanical Garden fifteen minutes walk away.
Tues-Sun 1-7 pm

Contemporary Arts Space (Espacio de Arte Contemporaneo)

Arenal Grande 1929, Aguada
Uruguay's premier public gallery located in an ex-prison is dedicated entirely to contemporary artists both Uruguayan and international. The exhibit changes three times a year. Guided visits are available in English by writing to visitas@eac.gub.uy. Combine with a visit to the Palacio Legislativo or the Tristan Narvaja market on Sundays.
Wed-Sat 2-8 pm (3-9 pm during the summer season), Sun 11-5 pm

Montevideo Photography Centre (Centro de Fotografia de Montevideo)

18 de Julio 885, Centro
Located in the historic Bazar Building, the CDF promotes photography as a way to provoke debate and critical thinking about Uruguayan identity and social issues. They are the people who organise the sometimes provocative photo-galleries found outdoors in the Old City, Parque Rodó and Parque Prado.
Mon-Fri 10 am-7 pm, Sat 9.30-2.30 pm

Museo Torres García

Sarandí 683, Ciudad Vieja
Joaquín Torres García (1874-1949) is Uruguay's most internationally renowned artist, responsible for the infamous image re-visioning the Americas with South America at the head. Born in Montevideo, he spent his formative years in Europe working with art giants like Picasso. Returning home, Torres García dedicated his life to teaching and developing his theory of Constructive Universalism, catalysing the development of abstract art in South America, and drawing connections between pre-Columbian art and European modernism. The museum has three floors of exhibition space, educational activities and art workshops and a wonderful book and gift shop on the ground floor.
Mon-Sat 10 am-6 pm

Museo Gurvich

Sarandí 522, Ciudad Vieja
José Gurvich (1927-1974) was born in Lithuania and moved to Uruguay as a child. He was part of the controversial studio created by Torres Garcia, where he worked until it closed. In 1970 he moved to New York where he died at the height of his career, aged 47.
Mon-Fri 10 am-6 pm, Sat 10 am-3 pm

Art collectives

Pera de Goma
On the corner of Ciudadela and Soriano, Ciudad Vieja
This effervescent new gallery showcases emerging artists and artists who have been around for longer but are not part of the traditional gallery scene. Well worth a visit.
Thurs-Fri 5-9 pm, Sat 4-8 pm

Centro Cultural Marte
Florida 1215, Centro
Another artists collective with a gallery. Directed by Gustavo Tabárez (he speaks English).
Wed-Fri 2-6 pm, Sat 10 am-6 pm

Fundación de Arte Contemporaneo (FAC)
Maldonado 1273, Centro
Artists collective directed by Fernando López Laje. Avant-garde, video art. Opening hours unavailable.

CasaMario
Piedras 627-9, Ciudad Vieja
An avant-garde collective with folks from multiple disciplines including dance, architecture and music. They do not have regular opening hours and can be contacted via Facebook as "Proyecto Casamario".

Commercial art galleries

Xippas
Bartolomé Mitre 1395, Ciudad Vieja
Xippas has galleries in Paris, Athens and Geneva as well as Montevideo. They sell work by high-level contemporary artists such as Brazilian collagist Vik Muniz.

Al Sur Taller de Cuadreria
Bartolomé Mitre 1379, Ciudad Vieja
Next door to Xippas is a small shop which specialises in framing the work of Uruguay's most successful artists. The salt-of-the-earth owner Hector Pérez has a small but impressive collection by well-known Uruguayan artists – many of whom are no longer with us – for sale.

Galeria SOA
Consituyente 2046 esq. J.M. Blanes, Parque Rodó

SOA concentrates on offering works by contemporary artists, the majority from Uruguay. Nice little exhibition space with a cafe in trendy Parque Rodó.
Mon-Fri 10 am-7.30pm, Sat 11 am-4 pm

Galeria Ciudadela
Sarandí 699, Ciudad Vieja
This gallery founded in 1982 sells works by Uruguayan artists – past and present.

Engelman Ost Collection
Rondeau 1426, Centro
A private collection featuring a wide number of contemporary artists. Email the owner Clara Ost at costlow@adinet.com.uy to request a visit as this gallery otherwise only opens to the public for specific events.

Historic cafes and bars

Let the history seep into your bones as you explore the real cafes and bars of Montevideo. These are some of the classic cafes and bars you can find dotted around the city. Not one of them is "for export" so you'll be contributing to the local economy, helping to keep alive places that are in constant danger of being closed down.

I've included hours where I could find them. Assume the rest to be open at midday and in the evening and closed Sundays. But as these places are run by their owners, they may potentially close on a whim, and definitely if there's a family barbeque (*asado*) invitation involved.

Oro del Rhin

Convención 1403 esq. Colonia, Centro
One of the most traditional cafes in the city. Famous for its strawberry pie (tarta de frutilla), Eisschokolade (a milkshake with chocolate, cream and ice cream) and Mozart coffee (with cognac, double cream and cinnamon).
Open: Mon-Sat, 8.30 am-8 pm.

Cafe Brasilero

Ituzaingó 1447, Ciudad Vieja
Founded in 1877 and frequented by famous writers like Mario Benedetti and Eduardo Galeano before their demises. The lighting is reminiscent of the days of gaslight.
Open: Mon-Fri 9 am-8 pm, Sat 9 am-4 pm

Cafe Misiones

Corner of Misiones and 25 de Mayo, Ciudad Vieja
Emblematic green antique-tiled frontage on a busy corner of the Old City.
Open: Mon-Fri 7.30 am-6 pm.

Tasende

Ciudadela 1300 esq San Jose, Centro
Founded in 1931, located just off the Plaza de Independencia, the Tasende was frequented by presidents and known as the backrooms of power. I'm not sure what's colder, the marble table tops or the treatment of the customers by the waiters. However, the *pizza al tacho* (pizza base and grilled cheese, no tomato sauce) and cold beer go down a treat.

Clube Brasileiro

18 de Julio 994, 2nd floor (take the elevator), Centro
The 100-year old Clube Brasileiro, pictured at the start of this article, is actually a restaurant in a social club. The surroundings are incredible – stained glass windows, art-deco mosaic floors, decorative fireplace, a billiard table (no touching!). They serve breakfast, lunch and early dinners including fresh fruit smoothies (*licuados*, though the menu says "jugos" erroneously).
Open: Mon-Sat 8 am-9 pm.

Bar Montevideo Sur

Paraguay 1150, esq Maldonado, Palermo
Opened in the1930s, the bar is untouched by time, despite the fact that its owners have refused a number of offers to update the place. In its heyday it was frequented by journalists and police. Montevideo used to be full of bars like this. Order a beer and don't be put off by the drunk locals - they are entirely harmless!

Los Yuyos

Luis A de Herrera 4297 esq. Cubo del Norte, Prado
Founded in 1906, this classic bar in the leafy neighbourhood of el Prado is famous for its spirits flavoured with herbs (*yuyos* is a colloquial term for herbs). At one time there were more than 200 flavoured liqueurs, all identifiable simply by their colour, before someone decided to start labelling the bottles in the 1970s.

El Sol de Jacinto Vera

Juan Paullier 2946, Jacinto Vera
Soak up deepest Montevideo in this picturesque bar with even more picturesque locals in this very residential neighbourhood.

Beaches

Montevideo has ten beaches[18], all with fine white sand. Montevideans just love the rambla and their beaches, and flock to them all year around. Parque Rodó, Pocitos, Malvin and Carrasco have their own beaches but any beach is accessible by bike, bus or walking in minutes. It took me over 12 years of living in Montevideo before I actually started to go to the beach. I was turned off because it always struck me that a city beach is not the cleanest. However, I've become a convert over the past few summers and feel very happy to recommend them.

Water quality Always an important issue in a city beach. Montevideo's beaches are monitored to international standards. During high season, water quality information is published in the media. In case of a water quality issue, the lifeguard stations fly a red flag with a green cross in the centre. The local government suggests avoiding swimming 24 hours after heavy rains.

Sunscreen warning Between November and April, even on cloudy days, remember to wear sunscreen and a hat when out walking, even if just for 15 minutes. You don't want to get sunburned on your first day and have to stay in the shade the rest of your stay. And follow Montevideans and stay out of the sun between noon and four.

Playa Ramírez, Parque Rodó

A broad sandy beach right on the edge of Parque Rodó and two fun fairs, so plenty to do if you get bored of the sand. Very shallow water so ideal for children. Great little fish and chip stand at the far end called El Morrito. Great sunset viewing. Wheelchair accessible. Buses: Any to Parque Rodó

Playa de los Pocitos, Pocitos

Known locally simply as "Playa Pocitos", it's a long wide beach with lovely white sand popular with the middle-class residents. Reasonably deep so good swimming. Bordered by apartment buildings (think Tel Aviv or Nice) which cast a long shadow over most of the sand the last few hours of the

18The word for beach in Spanish is *playa* – prounounced *ply-zhah* in "Uruguayan".

day. Several *paradores* (stands) selling snacks and cold drinks. There's a beach football stadium set up during the summer. Wheelchair accessible.

Puerto de Buceo

This little beach looking out towards the marina (pictured directly above) is not apt for swimming (a water quality issue). I include it here more for the jetty. It makes a pleasant walk from Pocitos though.

Playa Buceo and Playa Malvin

Buceo is a wide very flat beach typically used for sports. Combine with a visit to the Buceo Cemetery (Montevideo's undiscovered rival to Buenos Aires' famous Recoleta Cemetery) which overlooks the water. See *Outdoors*. Malvin is a wide very flat beach typically used for sports, especially kite-surfing. A resto-style *parador* serves meals and drinks. Wheelchair accessible.

Playa Honda, Punta Gorda

A smallish beach with white sands with deeper waters than others (hence the name *honda* meaning deep). A petrol station across the road does a roaring trade in cold drinks and snacks. The one beach in Montevideo where a surfer might find some waves.

Playa de los Ingleses, Punta Gorda

Can get very busy during summer and given that it is small, you feel the crowds more than you will elsewhere. The Punta Gorda and Carrasco sports club overlooks the beach and has a restaurant with a large terrace. The Fair Sailing Centre attached to the club offers sailing and wind-surfing lessons and boat and board hire at very competitive prices. See *Outdoors*

Tours and guided visits

Montevideo has a number of tours. Unfortunately, tour guides are still trained to reel off historic facts about monuments and museums while dressed impeccably rather than dig into history, geography and anecdotes to really bring their subjects to life.

The good news is that a number of private initiatives are emerging to offer more engaging tours so for now I am just recommending the tours that either have been highly recommended to me by my guests or that I have done myself and liked a lot.

Wine tours

These tours will give you a real feel for Uruguay, where you will be guided by Ryan, a South African and your very own inside man and wine expert, who has been living in Uruguay for five years and who knows all the best places. Besides tasting great wines and various expressions of the famous Tannat grape (now considered the healthiest wine in the world) you will get to meet real people behind the scenes, who will share their passion and love for wine-making. A bunch of my guests at Casa Sarandi Guesthouse had taken tours with Ryan for several years before I ever met him. I was consistently impressed by their accounts of his creative approach to the tours – I could see he was matching vineyards and activities closely to the preferences of the visitors – with more rustic experiences for some, luxury vineyards for others. Visit The Wine Experience website[19]

Soccer history tour

Did you know that Uruguay has the football squad which has won more international tournaments than any other in the world? Not bad for a nation of three million. Take a tour through Uruguay's footballing past including the stadium where the first ever World Cup was played. It's a great way to

19 http://www.thewine-experience.com/

spend the afternoon, and I say that as someone who doesn't like football. You can visit Uruguay's national Football Museum in the Centenario Stadium by yourself; however, I recommend going with the fabulous Fanáticos Futbol Tours given that the museums have no English-language signage, and the fact that the Fanáticos are full of hysterical pearls of knowledge. Their regular tour goes to the Football Museum, the two stadiums where the first ever World Cup was played in 1930, and the museum of Uruguay's most popular team, Peñarol. Visit the <u>Fanáticos website</u>[20]

Sensorial city tour

A city tour in a comfortable van with cannabis tastings at three classic tourist destinations plus the kick of getting to smoke a joint on the steps of Uruguay's Legislative Assembly. The tour begins on the banks of the River Plate in Parque Rodó with a panoramic view of the city. You'll hear about the history of marijuana legalisation in Uruguay and partake of the first tasting. The tour continues to a nearby grow-shop. For most visitors the most fascinating aspect will be the astronomical prices of the pot paraphernalia. Next stop, the Legislative Assembly where the historic law was signed. Compare this to Colorado, USA where pot may be legalised but virtually impossible to smoke in most public places. The tour ends in the Old City at the port market, which The Guardian infamously called Disneyland for carnivores, just in time to calm your munchies. Find out more about <u>MVD High</u>[21]

Cannabis culture tour

This tour takes you to one of Montevideo's 12 growing coops where, if you are lucky, your guide may be one of the principal lobbyists behind the marijuana legislation. The cooperative is in an art-deco building in a residential neighbourhood of Montevideo. I got a chance to accompany Doug, a 60-something professional from Ontario, who is a member of a growers' club back home.
Doug really wanted to find out about the legislation and how implementation is going. His tour of the grow shop and growers' cooperative was led by Marco, a comparative lit professor and an incredibly knowledgeable guide to Uruguay's cannabis culture. After a tour of the cooperative, over his marijuana of choice, Doug got to sit down and quiz Marco, and I was impressed by the technical level of the conversation. This personal contact is the difference that Uruguay can offer you – a personal experience, not a homogeneous commercialised tour. Before he took his seat on the comfy sofa, Doug beamed at me and said, "This is going to be the best stone of my life!" Find out more about <u>MVD High</u>[22]

Both cannabis tours include tastings of top-grade produce, just as you would experience on a good wine tour.
Find out more about <u>cannabis legislation in Uruguay and how it affects visitors</u>[23]

---

20 http://www.futboltours.com.uy/
21 http://guruguay.com/uruguay-marijuana-tours/
22 http://guruguay.com/uruguay-marijuana-tours/
23 http://guruguay.com/foreigners-marijuana-uruguay/

Uruguayan soccer game experience

Your chance to see the beautiful game in action with zero stress. Fanáticos Futbol Tours will procure tickets, pick you up at your hotel, provide snacks and knowledgeable (and fun) bilingual guides and drop you off at your hotel at the end of the game. Games offered include internationals, local games and the big cups. What's unique about the football scene in Montevideo, versus Buenos Aires, is that everyone knows everyone else and you can get access that would be impossible elsewhere. So for instance, the Fanáticos have been able to arrange visits to training events at the local Liverpool Club for British Liverpool FC fans or for a fan to meet a Uruguayan footie idol. The grounds are also special, including the stadiums where the first ever World Cup was played, venues with river views and others in lovely green surroundings. And I would even recommend going to a soccer game even if you don't like football. Why? Because not only will you be soaking up a real cultural phenomenon, you'll have a captive Uruguayan next to you for 3-4 hours whom you can grill with all those burning questions you've been dying to ask since you arrived! Contact Nacho and Franco at info@futboltours.com.uy

Carnival and candombe culture tour

In conjunction with the Carnival Museum, this tour run by German-American Christine takes you to visit a local *comparsa* (drum and dance group) and accompany them during their weekly rehearsal in the heart of Montevideo. The tour starts with a visit to the Museo del Carnaval where you'll get an introduction to the history and evolution of Uruguayan Carnival. There are two options, going on public transport like the locals or in a private vehicle. Those choosing the private option get a short tour of the most important carnival sights in Montevideo before reaching the Mi Morena Cultural Centre. At the centre you will be welcomed by the group members and be able to observe how the dancers and typical *comparsa* characters rehearse. After a short introduction to the different drums that are played, you'll take to the street and accompany the *comparsa* on their regular Saturday night rehearsal parade. This is a real slice of Montevidean life, as these parades happen all over the city every night of the week.

To set up a tour contact Christine at experience@uruguay-autentico.com.
Also see *Museums*

Touring the Solis Theatre, Uruguay's oldest theatre

Buenos Aires, just off the Plaza de Independencia, Ciudad Vieja

The Teatro Solis (say it tay-AA-tro sol-EES), Uruguay's oldest working theatre, was inaugurated in 1856 and refurbished and reopened in 2004. There is a lively 30-minute tour to all the secret parts of the building as well as the two theatres and backstage. Visit the theatre in the morning to find out what time the English tour is that day and while you are it, why not check the box office for shows, which are very affordable. Tickets are often available until the last minute (Box office Tues-Sat 11 am-8 pm, Sun-Mon 3-8 pm. Reservations are not accepted). The theatre has a lovely gift shop, a good cafe and a top-of-the-range restaurant.

Tours are Tuesdays and Thursdays at 4 pm, Wednesdays, Fridays and Sundays 11 am, 12 noon and 4 pm, Saturdays at 11 am, 12 noon, 1 pm and 4 pm, and cost 50 pesos.

Art–deco & architecture tours

Montevideo has stunning architecture. I read somewhere that after New York, Montevideo is the city with most Art Deco buildings in the world. I always tell people to take a walk along the main avenue, 18 de Julio – not for the street itself but to keep looking up – the architecture is Belle Epoque, Art Deco, modernist. Even the Montevideo police HQ is an absolute Art Deco treasure! Tours Art Decó is run by a number of local architects with an interest in guiding anyone interested in art, design, architecture, history, preservation, urban planning and community development. The great thing about this being Montevideo is that your guide will blag you into a number of places that are generally closed to the public.
Contact Marta via the Tours Art Decó website[24]

Palacio Salvo visit

Montevideo's most iconic building (pictured above), right on the Plaza de Independencia, was inaugurated in 1928 and was the highest building in South America until 1935. The views are stunning and as a home to almost one thousand people, Salvo is practically a "vertical barrio". Palacio Salvo has a twin, the Palacio Barolo in Buenos Aires. However, because the BA cousin is on Avenida de Mayo surrounded by other enormous buildings, it does not dominate the landscape like Salvo does in Montevideo. One-hour-long tours for 2-10 people have just started operating in English on Wednesdays at 11 am, 12 noon and 1 pm until March, and then at 11 am from April to October. You can just show up but if you want to ensure a spot send an email to experience@uruguay-autentico.com. Plan to arrive 15 minutes early to pay the tour fee of 200 pesos.

If you just want to enjoy the **view from the viewing deck on the 25th floor**, a Spanish-speaking escort will take 2-10 people up there at 10.30 am, 11.30 am and 12.30 daily until the end of March and the same times from Fridays to Sunday between April to October. Daily visits will resume at the end of the year. The viewing deck visit costs 100 pesos per person.

Legislative Palace (Palacio Legislativo)

The seat of Uruguay's government is a wonderfully preserved palace inaugurated in 1925 when Uruguay was a rich nation. Decorated with fine marbles, wooden carvings, curved glass and murals, one visitor called it "the most beautiful building in South America". There is a great little tour which runs twice a day where you'll get to visit the building and find out more about Uruguay's unusual political system. The tour in English is Monday-Friday at 10.30 am and 3 pm and lasts around 45 minutes. Go to the back entrance on Av. General Flores. As the Palace is a little off the beaten track, combine this with a visit to the Agricultural Market (see *Architecture*) or the ECA art gallery (see *Art Galleries*).

---

24 http://www.toursartdeco.com/

Jewish culture tour

This tour is for people who'd like to get an overview of the city of Montevideo as well as a feeling for the Montevideo which is home to 14,000 Jewish people. Their ancestors arrived in the 1920s principally from Germany and Hungary and became an integral part of Montevidean society. The tour takes you to a number of neighbourhoods to visit the first synagogue in Montevideo and other Jewish community buildings. A British visitor told me that he felt the most interesting part was the visit to a community centre in Pocitos which houses a synagogue, a *yeshivah* (religious study group) and a "very tasty bakery". Your guide tells some of the history of the various Jewish communities as the tour progresses and also points out non-Jewish sites of interest. Visit the Jewish Tours website[25]

City tours

I don't recommend the tourist bus tour that goes around the city unless you like that kind of thing and you have just one day in town. Montevideo is small enough that most places are visitable on foot or you could take a bus yourself (for less than a dollar) if you'd like to go further afield. The tour focuses on dropping people on and off at shopping malls and guests of mine have complained that the bus drives too quickly.

I am a little reluctant to recommend a tour that relies on tips to pay its guides. This is the case of the **Free Walking Tour** organised by the Football Fanatics, which starts from the foot of the statue of General Artigas on his horse at the Plaza de Independencia on weekdays at 11 am and 2 pm on Saturdays. However, guests tell me that the tours are pretty interesting and of course you can tip generously, right?

---

25 http://www.jewishtours.com.uy/

Day trips

Just 10 minutes from the centre of Montevideo you can get to world-class vineyards, half an hour and you are in 20,000 hectares of ecological wetlands, in an hour at gorgeous white sandy beaches and in just over two hours in a Portuguese-founded UNESCO heritage site.

My recommendations for day trips go from the closest to the furthest from Montevideo. And remember you don't need to hire a car, you can take the bus – they are just so frequent, comfortable and even have Wi-Fi!

Vineyards around Montevideo

Uruguay has been producing great wines over the last decade or so, winning international prizes in the red Tannat category particularly. Vineyards are just 10-15 minutes from the centre of the city. A French guest who sells oak barrels stayed at our guesthouse for a week and visited 17! At the end of her stay, we asked her recommendation and she chose Bodega Bouza which offers tours in English and a truly excellent restaurant. Check the Bouza website and book your tour before you go (check that they are not receiving a tour group at the same time for the nicest experience). Take a taxi, getting an idea the price before you get in. The ride takes literally 12 minutes and it costs around 450 pesos one way to go to Bouza from the Old City. Bouza will call a cab for you to get back to the city.

Santa Lucia Wetlands – horse-riding and bird-watching

Half an hour's drive from Montevideo lie the wetlands of the Santa Lucia River, a nature reserve where a unique ecosystem is produced by the tides of the River Plate flowing in and out of the flatlands around the mouth of the Santa Lucia River, creating a salt-water wetland environment. There is wonderful array of biodiversity, tiny islands, streams and creeks. I would recommend hiring locals to take you around. Costa Llana is located close to the wetlands and offers bird-watching and horse-riding on the beach. They have English-speaking guides and can arrange transfers to and from Montevideo. The Costa Llana website gives good instructions on how to arrive by public transport.

Atlántida – lovely beach just one hour's drive away

Atlántida[26] is a sleepy resort town, 45 km east of Montevideo. We love to go there around midday, especially during a sunny day off-season. The beaches are completely deserted in the winter months. Go for a long walk along the wide, white, pine tree-lined beach. Walk west (facing the sea, to the right) until you get to a house in shape of an eagle's head. Back in town, pig out at Restaurante Don Vito. Order the grilled lamb (*cordero*) or *bife ancho* (a cut usually reserved for export). Amazing desserts too. Buses go from Tres Cruces.

Piriápolis (and Punta Colorada) – art-deco beach town

Piriápolis[27] has a long promenade dominated by an art-deco hotel which was the largest resort of its time in the whole of South America when it was built in 1930. You feel like you are stepping back to a gentler time. The beach is flat and the water shallow for paddling. The founder of Piriápolis, Francisco Piria, was an alchemist and laid out the streets of the city in a precise geometric design to harness bioenergy. You can walk out of town 5 km to Punta Colorada and the first truly Atlantic waters. The skyscrapers you see in the distance are Punta del Este. There are very occasional buses from Punta Colorada back to Piriápolis – or you can enjoy walking back into the sunset. Buses leave Tres Cruces for Piriápolis every 30-60 minutes and take 1.5 hours.

Punta del Este – glamorous beach city with off-season charm

In the 1950s, "Punta" was the running ground of Brigitte Bardot, Frank Sinatra and his Rat Pack. In recent years surrounding towns have had a come-back and seen visitors as diverse as Shakira, Martin Amis and Mark Zuckerberg. It's two long beaches lined with high rises, it's the centre of South American glamour magazines and cheesy TV shows during the summer, and heaves with Argentinians and Brazilians in January and February. Off-season Punta del Este[28] has a very special charm. Head to the port and walk along the piers to fish sellers and huge seals basking next to the yachts. And do have a wander around the old peninsula above the port – it's a very different, low-rise Punta. Between June and October, it's often possible to see whales and dolphins from the

---

26 http://guruguay.com/atlantida-beach/
27 http://guruguay.com/piriapolis-punta-colorada/
28 http://guruguay.com/should-i-visit-punta-del-este/

coast[29]. Buses go from Tres Cruces every half an hour. Catch the ones that take 2 hours.

Colonia – UNESCO World Heritage Site

Colonia[30] was founded by the Portuguese in 1680. The historic quarter is full of old stone houses and cobbled streets. It is popular with visitors from Buenos Aires so avoid going on weekends if you want to experience the tiny city at its best. It's a great place for gift shopping and has a wide selection of quaint eateries. Colonia is small so you can easily explore it in 4-5 hours including lunch. Go swimming in the river off the pure white sandy beaches. Buses go from Tres Cruces every hour or less and take between 2.5 and 3 hours.

---

29 http://guruguay.com/whale-watching/
30 http://guruguay.com/colonia/

Outdoors

Outdoor living is a big part of Montevidean life. This is something I love about the city. Montevideans love to eat and drink in the open-air, so when Uruguay became the fourth country in the world to ban smoking indoors in public places No one really had much problem adapting to the new legislation and street-side cafes blossomed. People flock to the beach at the first sign of sunny weather. The rambla is full of people day and night with Montevideans of all ages hanging out there, drinking mate in the afternoons and in the evenings a cold beer.

So when you are here, make sure that you too make time for the outdoors.

Biking, running and walking along the rambla

The **rambla** is Montevideo's fifteen-mile (25km) boardwalk and Montevideans spend many of their waking hours there, walking, running, cycling, and drinking mate of course. It's safe to stroll at any time of the day or night. The rambla is at its most picturesque from the Old City (starting at the NH Colombia Hotel), and then heading east towards Parque Rodó (km 4.5), plush Pocitos beach (km 8), Buceo and the cemetery (km 10.5) and right to Carrasco (km 20). There are signposts every half km.

Bike rentals You can rent bikes all over Montevideo. Here are two companies that my guests have used and found reliable. Both companies will deliver bikes free of charge. Note that they may not be absolutely punctual.
Orange Bikes, Perez Castellano 1417, Ciudad Vieja Tel. 2908 82 86 orange.bike@hotmail.com Open 9.30 am-5 pm every day.

Bicicleteria Sur, Florida 1205 *esquina* Canelones Tel. 2901 0792 bicicleteriasur@gmail.com Open Monday-Friday 9 am-7 pm, closing for lunch from 1-3 pm. Saturdays 10-2 pm. Closed Sundays.

Parque Rodó – the park, the funfair, Sunday drumming, sunset

A helter skelter was the first fairground ride to appear on the banks of the River Plate 125 years ago. Ten years later, the 42 hectare park was landscaped by two French architects. By 1904, there was an artificial lake and a fairytale-style castle. Nowadays Parque Rodó (*par-kay roh-DOH*), which is also the name of the surrounding neighbourhood, is the park with most **statues** and monuments in the whole of the city. Stroll the park during the day with hundreds of mate-drinking locals. The waterside **funfair** is a **step back to a kinder, gentler time** for both children and adults. Montevideo's largest art collection, the **National Museum of Visual Arts**, is housed in the park and open every afternoon till 7 pm except Mondays (See *Art galleries*).

On **Sunday afternoons** a huge Brazilian **samba drumming** troupe plays for hours. Then around 7-8 pm, you can join La Melaza, Montevideo's only all-woman **candombe drumming** group, at their weekly open-air drumming session on the corner of on Blanes and Gonzalo Ramirez streets by the steps. Just follow the sound of drums and go with time to spare. These things are never punctual. And you MUST watch the **sun go down over the River Plate from Playa Ramirez** at least one day you are in Montevideo. See <u>Guru'Guay on Parque Rodó</u>[31]

Playa Ramirez – sundown and fish & chips

7pm on a summer's evening. The sun will be going down in under an hour. Where's the best spot to kick back and watch the sun go down over the city skyline? It's time for deep-fried fish and ice-cold beer at El Morrito in Playa Ramirez. El Morrito has a couple of tiny shacks selling sea food and drinks, overlooking the water to the left of the beach when you face the River Plate. We recommend you ignore everything else and order the *postas* – fillets of fresh white fish caught earlier that day, dipped in batter and deep-fried until they are wonderfully crispy and deliciously hot inside. Then walk home to wherever you are staying along the rambla.

Parque El Prado – botanical gardens, architectural glories

The Prado Park, known as El Prado, was the summer vacationing ground of Montevideo's elite in the late 1800s. The neighbourhood is full of **mansions**, some still glorious but most falling into rack and ruin. In the middle of this decadence is El Prado Park and Montevideo's **Botanical Gardens** which my mother politely described as "wild". Here is none of the prissiness of European botanical gardens. The plants and foliage are winning in their bid to overwhelm the buildings and greenhouses. The gardens are lovely shady place to escape to on hotter days and perfect for a visit after admiring the **Blanes Art Museum**, a fifteen minute walk away or before taking tea at the **Hotel del Prado**, inaugurated in 1912 (See *Architecture*). The surrounding neighbourhood is safe for strolling and definitely recommended for those who like to wander off-the-beaten-track. Botanial Garden opening hours: Every day 7.30 am-6.30 pm.

---

31 http://www.guruguay.com/parque-rodo-montevideos-oldest-park

Buceo Municipal Cemetery – Montevideo's best-kept secret

The Recoleta Cemetery in Buenos Aires is world-famous, but incredibly Montevideo's equivalent, the Buceo Cemetery is in my opinion even more **striking** and virtually unknown. An Italian photographer friend of mine came over to Montevideo, just to take shots of the **larger-than-life marble sculptures** - many brought over from Italy a century ago. The tombs are surrounded by exuberant palms and other **greenery** and there's a view of the river! It is a 30-minute bus ride from the city centre and is open from 8am to 5pm each day. Next door the British cemetery is less extravagant but has interesting tombstones including from the Second World War. Avenida Rivera 3934, Bus 142 (Costanera Estacion ANCAP)

Full Sailing – boat trips, windsurfing and kayaking classes & rental

What a great way to see Montevideo, from the water. Full Sailing, located on the border between the Carrasco and Punta Gorda neighbourhoods, is Montevideo's only sailing centre to offer classes and boat rentals to anyone with or without experience, and without a membership card. You just pay for your **boat**, or **windsurf** board, or **kayak by the hour**, or you can hire an **instructor** and buy a **package** of lessons on a **schedule that suits your holiday plans**. It's the perfect option for any visitor to Montevideo, where most nautical clubs only cater to members. What's more, prices are really, really **affordable** – we're talking around 10 USD per hour for kayak hire and 20 USD for an hour-long boat-ride for up to three people. See Guru'Guay on Full Sailing[32]

Maroñas Horse-racing – a day at the races and art–deco

This spectacular **art-deco stadium** right out of a Scott Fitzgerald novel was recovered from its abandoned state and reopened in 2003. Horse races are held **every Sunday afternoon** and **sometimes on Fridays**. There is a small entrance fee. The track is right across town in a neighbourhood completely off the tourist track, the working class Maroñas barrio. You can get a bus (the 102 for instance) which takes 45 minutes from the city centre and drops you off right at the entrance. If driving following signs to the "hipódromo". There is a **classic derby on January 6** each year - the Grand José Pedro Ramírez Prize - starting 2 pm. Check the Maroñas website for meetings, as the racetrack is closed when races are not on. Note: The website programme shows races held elsewhere too. Mouse-over the calendar day to see if "Maroñas" appears.

Rainy days – Going to the movies

Sometimes it rains and outdoor options are not possible. In which case if you're not into art galleries, museums or shopping, Montevideo has a bunch of cinemas. Uruguayans take their cinema very seriously, which means that the good news is that English language films -other than films for younger children- are never dubbed. See Guru'Guay for Montevideo cinema details[33]

---

32 http://guruguay.com/montevideo-sailing
33 http://www.guruguay.com/going-to-the-movies-in-montevideo

Shopping and buying original gifts

Most Montevideans shop in their neighbourhood supermarket and then they cut costs by buying fruit and vegetables and cheap clothing in weekly pop-up markets (called *ferias*) that rotate around different neighbourhoods. A visit to a shopping mall (known colloquially as a "shopping") is more of a social event, especially to enjoy the air-conditioning during summer – i.e. there are often more people browsing than buying.

Where to shop

Montevideo's main street 18 de Julio, which goes from Plaza Independencia to Tres Cruces where the bus station is, was once the centre of commercial activity but is much less frequented today. There you'll find what you can buy in the shoppings at cheaper prices. And when you look up you'll see the most amazing architecture. So if you need to do regular shopping, support local business and go to "18" as it is called by the locals.

Markets If you are in Montevideo on a Sunday don't miss the **Tristan Narvaja flea and antiques market**. You can really find anything laid out on a blanket in this street fair which octopuses its way through the streets around Tristan Narvaja street on a Sunday morning from 9 am till about 2 pm depending on the weather. Locals may suggest you visit a couple of *ferias* on weekends – principally the Parque Rodó and Biarritz *ferias*. But frankly the stands are just not interesting to visitors – the items are usually inferior quality and prices are much higher than you would expect to pay in North America or Europe.

Shopping malls Back to the "shoppings", the principal ones in areas where you are likely to stay are Punta Carretas Shopping in Punta Carretas (doh!), Montevideo Shopping, on the dividing line between Pocitos and Buceo, and Tres Cruces Shopping, above the bus station. You will be likely to visit them to buy a mobile phone SIM card or to exchange money on weekends (they are the only places where you can exchange money on Saturday afternoons and on Sundays). The malls will be marked on any tourist map.

Commercial opening hours

Most shops open Monday to Friday 9 am-7 pm and Saturdays 9 am-1 pm. They do not close for lunch. Only shopping malls open seven days a week, and are open until 10 pm every night. Most other shops close on Saturday afternoon and reopen on Monday morning.

Typical Uruguayan souvenirs

- **Dulce de leche** A caramel paste that Uruguayans put on absolutely everything.
- **Alfajores** A chocolate-covered cookie with *dulce de leche* in the middle (of course) that my relatives in Wales have called the most delicious snack ever. You can buy them in presentation boxes of up to 12.
- **Woollens** Uruguayan wool is INCREDIBLE. However, you may find it's easier and cheaper to get hold of Malabrigo and other delicious wool lines in your own country.
- **Wine** It may be cheaper to buy at home but you won't have the selection you find here.
- **Leather goods** Don't expect them to be cheap, though – handbags, etc. are likely to be more expensive than you might find in Europe or North America
- **Mate set** During your time in Montevideo you'll see 99% of locals walking around sipping mate from a gourd with their thermos flask of hot water tucked firmly under their arm. So you'll think, wow, what a great idea, and buy a gourd and *bombilla* set – that will never be used again! At least not until a roving Argentine, Uruguayan, Paraguayan or Gaucho comes your way.

Shops which stock gift–worthy items

It's not easy to find great gifts in Montevideo. You have to remember here that the national market is small. The population of Montevideo is just 1.5 million people and a much smaller percentage of those people have disposable income for trinkets.

So let me remove the leg-work. I've come up with some suggestions of great shops where you can pick up original gifts that your friends and family might actually want. In most shops, gifts are usually gift-wrapped for you, which is a very nice touch.

Solis Theatre gift shop, Buenos Aires street just off the Plaza de Independencia, Ciudad Vieja
Lovely selection of art-deco posters of the 1930 World Cup, carnival, theatre; CDs of Uruguayan music; great selection of DVDs of Uruguayan films that you are unlikely to find anywhere else. Just off the Plaza de Independencia.

Torres Garcia Museum gift shop, Sarandi 683, Ciudad Vieja
T-shirts, bags, shot glasses, boxed sets of wine glasses, mugs – all engraved or painted with iconic Torres Garcia symbols. Absolutely charming and very reasonably priced.

La Pasionaria gift shop, Reconquista 587, Ciudad Vieja

Very original trinkets, designer clothing and books. Somewhat pricey but you'll love the stuff. Just behind the Solis Theatre.

Manos del Uruguay, various locations

Specialises in fine Uruguayan crafts, especially hand-crafted woollens. Watch out for their end-of-season sales when prices are often marked down 50% . The shawls and scarves are out of this world. They also carry ceramics by a number of more well-known local artists. There is an outlet at San Jose 1111 (check out deals upstairs). There are stores in the malls at Punta Carretas and Montevideo Shopping.

Tristan Narvaja flea and antiques market, the streets around Tristan Narvaja street, Centro

You can really find anything laid out on a blanket in this street-fair which octopuses its way through the streets around Tristan Narvaja street on a Sunday morning from 9 am till about 2 pm depending on the weather. Great buys are old ceramic tiles, tin soldiers, vinyl LPs, brass door knockers, old postcards and photos, antique glassware and on and on and on.

Llorach Vitrales (stained glass makers), Canelones 952, Barrio Sur

Hand-crafted stained glass ornaments and even windows from this little workshop. You can peruse designs on Mauricio's website: www.mauriciollorach.com and email him at contacto@mauriciollorach.com

Santerías (Umbanda religious objects)

These little stores sell artifacts used in the Umbanda religion – statuettes of Iemanjá the sea goddess, candles and other votive bits and pieces. Kitsch-lovers go wild for this stuff. Umbanda is a South American religion blending African traditions brought over by enslaved West Africans in the 1800s with Roman Catholicism and indigenous American beliefs. There are several santerías on the street surrounding Tres Cruces bus station. Or combine with a trip to the Palacio Legislativo (see *Tours*), as there are at least three santerías on Fernández Crespo street between 1715 and 1806.

Pecuari (leather)

Sells high quality leather clothing and bags. There are branches in Ciudad Vieja (Juan Carlos Gomez 1412), Carrasco (Arocena 1552) and Punta Carretas (Ellauri 591).

Olmos (tableware), Canelones 1993, Parque Rodó

Olmos produces the tableware used by middle-class Uruguayans. It's utilitarian but there are a couple of cute designs featuring the sun on the Uruguayan flag. Olmos is a company that the workers took over in the form a cooperative to keep their jobs.

El Tungue Le, Perez Castellano 1518, Ciudad Vieja

A quirky little shop selling vinyl records, CDs, musical instruments and objects for the home. There is even a vintage box-style record player used for playing the vinyl on. "More stylish than Shoreditch, London," declared a guest of mine. Close to the Port Market.

Shopping for wine-lovers

Uruguay is famous for its wine and you've probably already experienced that where you live it's hard to get your hands on more than a tiny selection. So wine is a pretty special gift.

If you're serious about your wine choices, or are taking back for someone that is, avoid the supermarkets and support some of the local wine cellars. Not only will you be getting good advice but you'll also get decent packaging. A wine-drenched suitcase is not fun.

You can also go beyond table wine with sparkling wines, dessert wines (there are top-quality Tannat liqueurs) and distilled liquors like grappa. Oh, and the national creation Medio y Medio, a crisp blend of Muscat wine with sparkling white.

Great little wine stores

Esencia, Sarandí 359, Ciudad Vieja Owner Estrella has more than six years experience retailing wines, good expertise, and good offers. You can also do wine-tasting there.

Los Horneros, Guayaqui 3322, Pocitos Young sommelier Adriana Rossi stocks national wines and craft beers and she's very knowledgeable.

Cachi, on the corner of Julio Herrera and Colonia, Centro Wines, liqueurs, national and imported. All premium quality.

Los Domínguez, on the corner of Paraguay and Colonia, Centro and also in Montevideo Shopping Mall A traditional store with lots of wine and knowledge.

Las Croabas, Rivera 2666, Parque Batlle Slightly off the beaten track for visitors but owner Benjamín Doño and his family are probably the winesellers who know Uruguayan wine better than anyone else in Montevideo. You can find some real wine gems there.

Iberpark in the malls at Tres Cruces, Portones, the Mercado Agricola and other locations This is a convenience store but the assistants tend to be helpful and there are plenty of wines to choose from.

Buying online If you are in Montevideo for several days and plan your purchase in advance, visit the VinosUY website[34]. Owners Mario and Magdalena have the largest offer and best prices and will deliver to your hotel. They have confirmed to me that written English is no problem!

---

34 http://www.vinosuy.com/wineshop.php

Carnival

Montevideo has the world's longest carnival – it goes on for 40 days between the last week of January and, depending on the weather, the first days of March.

As it's virtually unknown to people outside of Uruguay, you are going to be able to experience one of the most authentic carnivals in the world.

What's so special about carnival in Montevideo?

Carnival – spelled *carnaval* in Spanish – is such an integral part of Uruguay's music and culture that **you can experience carnival preparations any day of the week all year round**. The drumming *comparsas* are out on the street practising every week, *murga* rehearsals are open to the public, and if you get really lucky the most popular *murgas* occasionally present shows from previous years in theatres. And contemporary artists like Jaime Roos and Pitufo Lombardo fuse carnival sounds into their music.

Because of an overshadowing by the Rio carnival plus a lack of information in English, there are **very few tourists** at carnival events, other than a few Argentinians and Brazilians. So events are **never too crowded** and it's a **totally local experience**.

Unlike Rio, it's also a **family-oriented** experience. Kids run around unsupervised, get their faces painted and find you at the end of the evening. Twenty-somethings hang out with their friends over a beer. Families bring picnic blankets and deck chairs to some of the bigger venues.

Plus it's **very affordable**. Seats for the parades cost around 10 USD, and the cost is the same or less for the *tablados*. *Tablados* in some neighbourhoods are even subsidised by the government with seats for 2 USD. You can buy fairground-style food and drink at reasonable prices.

Carnival 2016 dates

January 21 **Inaugural Carnival Parade** (*Desfile inaugural*) down 18 de Julio Avenue
January 25 **Tablados start across the city for the next 40 nights** *Tablados* are nightly shows featuring between 4 and 7 carnival groups.
February 4 and 5 **Las Llamadas** The amazing Llamadas Parade down Isla de Flores street between Barrio Sur and Palermo

The dates of carnival change each year, but what is guaranteed in Montevideo is that from the first day it's going to go on for **FORTY nights** – longer if it rains.

Uruguayan carnival traditions

Montevideo's carnival roots come from traditions brought from Africa and Spain. Nowadays it is organised around a competition where different groups compete in different carnival categories. The competition takes place in the parades and in the Summer Theatre (*Teatro de Verano*) but most people go to watch carnival in the *tablados*, outdoor carnival stages, in different parts of the city. The **most popular genres** are the *murgas* and the *comparsas*.

The *comparsas* are similar to the samba schools of Brazil, with dancers and drummers and flag bearers juggling enormous flags. Each *comparsa* can have almost a hundred drummers. However, stock characters are part of Uruguayan *comparsas* which you would never find in the Brazilian version: the *Gramillero* ("herb doctor"), an old guy with a bad back, the *Mama Vieja* ("old lady"), a fat lady in a huge dress, and *El Escobero* (the "Broomsman"), who performs extraordinary feats of juggling and balance with his broom. The dancers are also less "streamlined", shall we say, than Brazilian samba dancers. It's **so** refreshing. Carnival in Uruguay is all about having a good time and not about physical perfection.

A *murga* is a type of street performance. *Murgas* have Spanish roots but have evolved into something quintessentially Uruguayan. Each 17-person *murga* mixes song, theatre and comedy. Political satire and social commentary are a big part of the shows of the most popular murgas – and the audience will be falling around at the jokes referring to Uruguay's political class or relations with its Argentine neighbours. However, there's sufficient skill in the four-part harmonies and the extravagant costumes and make-up to keep any audience member enthralled.

The *Llamadas* (Spanish for "calls") are another great reason to visit Montevideo's carnival. These hugely popular drum parades feature tens of *comparsas*, and are the main attraction for visitors and locals alike. The tradition was started by the descendants of Africans who had been brought to Uruguay as slaves. And the *comparsa* drummers often wear costumes such as sun hats and black face-paint that they consider to reflect the music's historical roots in the slave trade. Uniquely, the procession take place through Isla de Flores, a tiny little narrow street in Barrio Sur, the heart of the former slave neighbourhood. Isla de Flores was chosen deliberately because the sound of the drums reverberates from one side of the street to the other at lightning speed, building the sound to an almighty crescendo. It's really something.

Essential carnival terms

Desfile – parade
Llamadas – literally means calls, but refers to the Llamadas Parade
Tablado – carnival stages which open every night in neighbourhoods across the city, sometimes specially constructed and sometimes in sports clubs and venues.
Murga – musical street-theatre group mixing social commentary and comedy
Cuerda de tambores – a candombe drumming troupe
Comparsa – the drumming troupe plus samba-style dancers
Entradas – tickets
Platea and **tribuna** - the types of seating in a tablado. Platea seats are numbered and closer to the stage. The tribuna is in the bleachers and cheaper.

The Guru's Carnival recommendations

- ✔ **The Llamadas** Absolutely amazing. Don't miss them.
- ✔ **The tablado shows** With a good recommendation you are going to love this. Check the Guru recommendations for the best carnival shows daily around midday on the Guru'Guay Facebook page[35]. There's some great stuff and some terrible, cheesy stuff too, so it's essential you check ing before you decide which *tablado* to visit.
- ✔ **Rehearsals** Murga rehearsals go on throughout Montevideo all year but really crank up a notch in December and January. Each *murga* has a place where they meet to rehearse (a sports club, a social club, a bowling green, a street corner) and fans gather with a cold beer to watch the rehearsals. If you get frustrated by not understanding the lyrics then this will not be for you, but if you like to soak up local atmosphere definitely put it on your list.
- ✔ **The San Baltazar drumming comparsa procession on January 6** It's a pre-Llamadas. In 2015, 36 comparsa drumming troupes (known as cuerdas de tambores) took part.

---

35 https://www.facebook.com/guruguay1

✔ **Carnival shows** A number of *murgas* put on shows in theatres at other times of the year which will be on the Guru'guay Facebook page.

Mehhh

✗ **The inaugural carnival parade** is kind of cheesy and heavy on advertising banners. I don't really recommend it unless you happen to be in town and it's on.

✗ ***Tablados* dominated by *parodistas, humoristas* or *revistas*** These are carnival genres that I have not mentioned above because they are kind of cheesy – think sequins, choreographed dancing, schmaltzy songs.

✗ **The main competition in the Summer Theatre** This is where the competition judging takes place and each group gives a full performance. For hard-core carnival buffs only – the *tablados* are much more varied and fun for visitors.

Buying carnival tickets

Tickets for the Carnival Parade and the Llamadas go on sale usually around mid December. You can buy them in any Abitab store in Uruguay up until 5 pm the day before the event. Tickets are cheap – around 10 USD and under. They don't typically sell out until the day before.

***Tablado* tickets** can be bought at the event on the day at the venue. Some of the larger venues also sell through Abitab.

Buying online For the first time you can buy tickets in advance to the shows with an English-speaking guide through the Carnival Museum.

Wait, my guidebook says that the carnival holiday is another time!

That's right. Uruguay also has an official two-day public holiday known as Carnival. It is not when carnival takes place (though shows will be on then too).

More reading on Guru'Guay.com
Check out my articles on carnival[36], including where to buy tickets

---

36 http://guruguay.com/tag/carnival/

Tango dancing

The *milonga* – or tango salon– scene in Montevideo is much more friendly and less intimidating than in Buenos Aires. It is frequented by a small group of mainly locals. So when they see a new face, people will come up to you to find out what you are doing there and to ask you to dance! This is very different from the competitive atmosphere in Buenos Aires. There is also a lot more space on the dance floor, useful for beginners.

So if you are a beginner or intermediate dancer, Montevideo is definitely the place for you to improve your technique. There are at least two milongas, or tango salons, open every night of the week.

Days, times and costs of milongas

You can find a milonga to attend **any night of the week** in Montevideo.

Monday is the quietest day of the week with the Lunera milonga run by veterans Cristina and Oscar in the classic venue with the best floor in Montevideo, Joventango. The **busiest nights are Wednesdays and Thursdays** with three milongas every night to choose from.

On **Wednesdays** from October, you can dance in the open air at the Milonga Callejera. The same group that organises the Callejera organises a milonga on the **last Friday of every month** at the Agricultural Market – "everyone goes" says my friend.

Milongas start about 9.30 pm during the week and 10.30 on weekends, but most dancers don't get there on time. On the weekends most people arrive about 11 pm and dancing goes on till 4 am.

La Conjura Bar, a bit of a hippie joint, has tango dancing at **Sunday lunchtime** from 1.30 pm. You could combine this with a trip to the Tristan Narvaja flea and antique market in the morning.

Watching, not dancing

Watching milongas is **perfectly acceptable**. If you don't dance and want to see a **real Montevidean tango experience**, I'd recommend you go to Lo de Margot on a **Saturday** night anytime from 11 pm. Margot is the Grande Dame of Tango. She's in her 80s and you are dancing in her living room. You'll see her toothpaste in the bathroom. Yes, seriously.

If you want to **watch a class**, just say hi to the teacher and ask if it's okay to watch (*Hola, puedo mirar?*). In fact this is another difference from Buenos Aires, where you may be summarily kicked out if you aren't prepared to take the class.

Entrance fee to the milongas is usually charged at the door and it is modest, about 200 pesos. If you take a class before you will normally not have to pay for the milonga.

Tango classes

Classes happen prior to the milonga. They start punctually around **8 pm** but you should check with the tutor at the time of booking.

Group classes **cost** approx. 200 pesos per person. If you plan to take a number of classes, you can negotiate a discount (e.g. four classes for the price of three). Private classes can cost about 750 pesos. Classes may be charged at the beginning or the end of the class, and if you stay on for the milonga it is at no extra charge.

Recommended teachers include Oscar and Cristina at Joventango on Mondays. My contact recommends mostly younger teachers, particularly any class by Chenkuo Che, Andrea Giospi (Milongas Intimas), Gabriela Farias, Gustavo Imperial and Diego Bado (also at JovenTango). Omar at the Museo del Vino on Wednesdays just loves to teach foreigners.

Find a milonga

The Montevideo milonga calendar can change at any given time. There is no one place to go to get up-to-date information. Sigh.. I know. <u>Tango DJ Veronica Bares' website</u>[37] is one of the most up-to-

---

37 http://djverobares.wordpress.com/milongas-en-montevideo/

date and Vero is very quick to answer questions. As always with most cultural events in Montevideo, the most up-to-date information appears in individual milonga pages on Facebook.

- **CHE MADAME** Rodo 2380 esq. Bulevar Artigas, Parque Rodo (**Thursdays**)
  In a basement. Contact: 095 451 335, 099 881432, 2409 3109
- **CHEPAPUSA** San José 870 entre Convención y Andes, Centro (**Thursdays**)
  Good floor
- **ESPACIO CARDAPIO** Uruguay 966 esq. Rio Branco, Centro
  Interesting mix of hippie types as well as "tangueros de ley", home-made food, cheap wine
- **GARUFA** Carlos Gardel 967, Barrio Sur
  Small space, good teacher, starts early
- **JOVENTANGO** Aquiles Lanza 1290 esq. San Jose in the Mercado de la Abundancia, Centro
  (**Mondays, Wednesdays, Fridays and Sundays**)
  Montevideo's most classic milonga in a large market place with places to eat. Mondays are the most fun and dancing with Oscar is the cherry on the cake.Contact 2901 5561, 2908 6816
  joventango@hotmail.com
- **LA CAUTIVA** San Jose 885 (just once a month 7-10pm)
  Art-deco mansion, frequented by the very best dancers including from the National Ballet.
  Don't miss it.
- **LA CONJURA BAR** Tristan Narvaja 1634 (**Sundays midday**)
  One of the few milongas with live music to dance to
- **LA MILONGUITA DEL BRECHA** Aquiles Lanza 1201 esq. Canelones, Centro (**Tuesdays**)
  Very small, live music to dance to
- **LA MORDIDA TANGO CLUB** Daniel Muñoz 2049 esq. Defensa in Bluzz Live, Tres Cruces (**Tuesdays**)
- **LO DE MARGOT** Constituyente 1812 esq. Gaboto, Palermo (**Saturdays**)
  Hosted in the Gran Dame of Tango's living room, great floor, Margot's charm. Unmissable.
  Margot is one of the few milongas to stay open over holiday periods. Contact 2410 6230.
  lodemargot@hotmail.com
- **MILONGUITA ALEGRE** Acevedo Diaz 1527 esq. Branzen, Tres Cruces (**Thursdays**)
- *MILONGA CALLEJERA* (Open air milonga) Plaza Liber Seregni, Centro (**Wednesdays**)
  An institution in the open air. Free classes, free milonga and free-style dancing encouraged.
- **MUSEO DEL VINO** Maldonado 1150 esq. Gutierrez Ruiz. (**Wednesdays**)
  Contact 2908 3430 info@museodelvino.com.uy
- **PORQUE LA MILONGA ES NUESTRO MENESTER** Agraciada 2790 esq. Alfredo Garcia Morales (**Fridays**)
  Young people, in a wonderful old house that's falling to bits
- **PRACTILONGA** Dragones 3566 (**Wednesdays**)
- **VIEJA VIOLA** Paysandu 1615 esq. Roxlo (**Saturdays**)
  Frequented by "tangueros de ley"- old-style tango dancers who adhere strictly to the traditional codes.
  Go with a partner and don't expect to be invited to dance
  Contact 091 297 426 rosariogotan@hotmail.com
- **YUYO BRUJO** Blanes 1053 entre Durazno y San Salvador (**Sundays**)

Live music

Montevideo has the most amazing live music scene for any city of 1.5 million inhabitants. Any night of the week there will be great live music shows to choose from, from numerous genres.

I've made a selection of generally lesser-known artists (unless mentioned) who will just blow you away.

Tango

Nestor Vaz Quinteto An old-guard Piazzolla-influenced bandoneon player leads this wonderful quintet featuring crack violinist Matias Craciun. His latest album pays homage to three cities – Montreal, Amsterdam and Montevideo. Moving.

Cuarteto Ricacosa Tango quartet of young guys with attitude.

Maia Castro One of Uruguay's top-selling female artists, Maia's latest album consists mainly of self-penned tangos. Along with her contemporary style, this sets her apart from most tango musicians who tend to limit themselves to interpreting classic tangos. Live shows demonstrate her very Uruguayan affinity for rock, candombe and carnival.

Francis Andreu Singer whose gravelly voice belies the fact that she made her debut in her teens and was quickly taken under the wing of Argentinian tango diva Adriana Varela. Smoky.

Ricardo Olivera What can I say, this guy is the Tom Jones of Tango and I love him – voice, attitude, medallion and all.

Julio Cobelli Probably Uruguay's most well-known tango guitarist. Soulful.

Bajofondo Internationally successful electronic tango collaboration between Uruguayan and Argentinian artists.

Carnival and carnival fusion

Any murga (particularly the younger ones such as Agarrate Catalina, Queso Magro, Cayó la Cabra, Metele que Son Pasteles) *Murgas* are a big feature of any carnival show, so there'll be lots of options from the end of January to early March. The rest of the year, some *murgas* play live shows in theatres. You can also watch *murgas* rehearsing in any number of venues, all open to the public, particularly in December and January. See *Carnival*

Pitufo Lombardo Pitufo emerged from the carnival scene to mix carnival sounds with rock. He often plays with Ney Peraza, one of my favourite guitarists.

Jaime Roos Probably Uruguay's most successful contemporary artist with a trajectory dating from the 1970s when he was exiled in the Netherlands. His songs regularly become national anthems. Uplifting.

Candombe

Ruben Rada Much loved iconic singer and percussionist whose career starting in the 60s has had a major impact on contemporary Uruguayan music. A larger-than-life personality who has been involved in all sorts of musical genres, including a spoof soul album and children's shows.

La Ventolera Nineteen trombones, trumpets and saxes together with a full complement of candombe drummers, La Ventolera sings and dances its way through Uruguayan classics. Big smile-on-your-face factor.

Percussion

Nico Arnicho In the land of percussion, Nico (pictured above) is one of Uruguay's most outstanding. His long-running show Super Plugged in the Solis Theatre every Saturday night plugs a 30-person audience into the sound desk, transporting you to other landscapes.

Tatita Marquez Maximum exponent of candombe-fusion. A devotee of Hari Krishna, Tatita has mixed classic candombe (he's founded a bunch of comparsas) with electronic music and most recently Latin jazz. You might see a show of his in New York.

Any candombe comparsa on the street On any night of any day of the year, you may run into a comparsa of drummers and dancers practicing for the next carnival. **La Melaza**, an all-woman troupe, rehearses every Sunday from about 7 pm starting at the corner of Blanes and Muller streets just off Parque Rodó.

Latasónica Highly choreographed percussion band with an equal mix of men and women who play just about anything they can lay their hands on – pots and pans, plastic pipes with flip-flops, basketballs...

Latin

Rumberos MVD is a five-piece salsa and Cuban timba band. What makes them particularly Uruguayan is their repertoire –- they do salsa versions of local artists including Jaime Roos, Ruben Rada and tango idol, Carlos Gardel -- as well as Buena Vista Social Club covers.

Proyecto Mestizo is an eight-piece Afro-Latin roots band. All eight band members sing and their repertoire focuses on songs from the coasts of Colombia, Venezuela and Peru; Cuba and Puerto Rico; as well as Uruguay.

Sonora Borinquen Uruguayan tropical music fuses Caribbean rhythms salsa, plena and cumbia with Uruguayan murga and candombe. Sonora Borinquen is the most illustrious Uruguayan tropical music band in the country. Founded in 1964 and still going strong today, their leader was given the keys of the City of Montevideo in 2012 and a glossy picture book on the band today was published in 2015.

Tropical bands may play locales that can be somewhat dodgy if you don't blend in. However two contemporary soloists in the tropical scene, **El Gucci** and **Gerardo Nieto**, are artists who play more mainstream venues.

Rock and pop

Buenos Muchachos Dark rockers who inspire a loyal following. Singer Pedro Dalton is a multimedia artist in the vein of Tom Waits. You are more likely to catch a live show of their down-sized alter ego, Dos Daltons.

Mandrake Wolf Composer of great songs, owner of a kind of stringy voice, Mandrake gives a great live show when he's in the mood. He's been around for years but Uruguayan 20-somethings just love him.

Hermanos Láser One of the first bands to promote and sell their album solely online. Live, I love their great art work and visuals and the furious harmonica. Can you feel the Wilco influence?

Santullo Rock royalty here though he's never been particularly prolific. Aligned with the Bajofondo project, his hit "El Mareo" was nominated for a Latin Grammy for best alternative song. His album Bajofondo presenta Santullo was awarded a Uruguayan Grammy (the Graffitis) in 2009 in the electronic music category. Intense rock live shows.

Fede Graña y Los Prolijos Swept the boards of the 2014 Graffitis winning best song, best pop album and best cover art with their rock/polka/funk.

Samantha Navarro With nine albums to her credit, Samantha is one of my favourite singer-songwriters. Stunning voice. Great tunes. Great sense of humour which really comes over live.

4 pesos de propina A semi-anarchical music project emerging from hippie summers in Rocha, 4 pesos now packs major venues in Montevideo.

Folk and roots

Berta Pereira Explores the roots of Uruguayan music with a pared-down indigenous sound. Spine-chilling. Usually plays tiny venues.

Ana Prada The most internationally known face of Uruguay's folklore scene. Quirky and contemporary.

Sebastian Jantos Here is where you start to realise that Uruguay and Brazil are very close neighbours. At some point someone will discover Seba. Chill-out.

Ernesto Diaz As far as I know the first musician ever to record in Portunhol, the dialect that is spoken on the Uruguay-Brazil border in his native Artigas. Laid-back.

Fredy Perez More known for his guitar playing, a few years ago Fredy put out a solo album of more unusual tangos and folklore. I went to his live show with little expectation, only to find the hairs standing up on the back of my neck all the way through. Exquisite.

Maine Hermo New singer-songwriter whose first album was a beautiful little gem reminiscent of Julieta Venegas. The lyrics are pure poetry.

Trelew Uruguayan-Welsh collaboration with contemporary versions of Celtic songs and others. Debut album nominated for a Grafitti. OK, I'll confess. It's my band.

Instrumental

Club de Tobi String quartet which started their career on Sarandi street in the Old Town playing rock versions of anything from traditional Uruguayan folk to Bob Marley. Having developed a "Tobi" sound, they are hugely popular with a really enjoyable live show.

Mushi Mushi Orquestra This is River Plate alternative folk at its gypsy or circus-style best. Cheering.

Popo Romano Uruguay's most famous bass player is a frequent presence on the Montevideo live music circuit whether in his solo shows or accompanying other bands. He's an understated guy just as happy to do a gig with his pre-teen granddaughter Juli as to play at an improvisation festival in Paris. An experience.

Gustavo Ripa Member of two iconic 80s bands, several years ago guitarist Gustavo had the brilliant idea of recording his *Calma* series – solo albums playing well-known songs by Uruguayan composers on the guitar. Three platinum discs and several Graffiti awards later, his live show, often with Popo Romano, is an unexpectedly beautiful thing.

Montevideo's great live music venues

One of the best things about visiting Montevideo in my experience is the live music. For a country of three million, Uruguay has a huge amount of highly talented musicians playing a huge variety of music. And the good news for visitors is that chances are there will be a number of great shows on while you are in town, regardless of how short your stay may be.

Ticket prices are very affordable for local acts. You can easily pay less than 10 USD to see a world-class band close up.

Live music audiences in Montevideo are wonderfully mixed age-wise. So you can feel comfortable checking out any club regardless of your age. Uruguayans tend to dress down so jeans are fine absolutely anywhere, even at the theatre.

Remember this is Uruguay, so shows usually do not start until 9 pm at the earliest.

This is just a selection of the pubs, clubs and concert venues which offer live music on a regular basis.

Small intimate clubs

- Tractatus, Rambla 25 de agosto 540, Ciudad Vieja
  Shows almost every day in their little gold-seated theatre and in the restobar. Well worth a visit. Take a cab as the area can be a little dodgy in the evenings. www.facebook.com/CentroCulturalTractatus

- Museo del Vino, Maldonado esq. Héctor Gutierrez Ruiz, Barrio Sur
  My favourite place to watch world-class musicians close up, with a good glass of wine. Tango milonga on a Wednesday then live music from Thursday to Saturday nights inclusive. Music is mainly Uruguayan. www.facebook.com/Museo-del-Vino-cava-bar-boutique-de-vinos-114026305319187/

- La Conjura Bar, Tristán Narvaja 1634 esq. Uruguay, Centro
  A hippie bar featuring more Afro and Latin bands, lots of candombe with occasional visits from groups from outside of Uruguay. Shows start late, usually after 11 pm. Fridays and Saturdays. ww.facebook.com/conjura.bar/

- Paullier y Guaná, Paullier 1252, Parque Rodó
  Music in the basement, attracts some of the more well-known artists often playing down-sized sets. Plan to go earlier and eat in the former general store upstairs. Jam sessions with some of Uruguay's best musicians on Tuesday nights. Live music Tuesdays to Saturdays. www.facebook.com/paullieryguanarestaurantebar

- Kalima, Durazno 1952 esq. Jackson, Parque Rodó
  Live music usually in the tiny basement downstairs. There's a jazz "hot club" every Friday night from 11 pm. A social enterprise which works with people with disabilities. Provides a real service to the community as well as great music. Open every evening except Mondays. www.facebook.com/kalima.boliche

- Perillan, Juan D. Jackson 1083 esq. Durazno, Parque Rodó
  A retro restaurant which showcases well-known and often more avant-garde artists in their "Musica para gente linda" acoustic soloist series on Wednesday nights. Tango instrumentals on Friday nights over dinner. www.facebook.com/perillanuruguay

- El Mingus, San Salvador 1952 esq. Jackson, Parque Rodó
  Tiny little restobar which amazingly manages to squeeze in a band occasionally, though it can be hard to hear the music. Great food. Live music on Tuesdays and Wednesdays. www.facebook.com/el.mingus

- El Tartamudo, 8 de octubre 2545, Tres Cruces
  Used to have great bands every night of the week but their calendar seems fairly empty recently. Their website advertises live music on Wednesdays and Thursdays. Wed-Sat from 8 pm. www.eltartamudobar.com

- Joventango, in the Mercado de la Abundancia, San Jose esq. Aquiles Lanza, Centro
  This classic tango milonga regularly features live bands at their periodic cafe-concert evenings, typically held on Sundays and occasional Fridays. Shows start earlier than most – about 7.30 pm. www.facebook.com/joventango.institucion

- Sotovoche, Zum Felde 1662, Malvín
  Recently opened cultural centre with a great musical offering, food, wine and craft beers.
  - www.facebook.com/sotovoche

Small rock bars and venues

- Bluzz Live, Daniel Muñoz 2049 esq. Defensa, Tres Cruces
    Venue close to Tres Cruces bus station featuring mainly heavier bands.
- Solitario Juan, Rodó 1830 esq. Gaboto, Centro
    Small alternative rock bar with interesting line-ups.
- Shannon Irish Pub, Bartolome Mitre 1318, Ciudad Vieja
    Live music virtually every evening including Sundays. Mainly rock, blues, Celtic and covers.
- Pony Pisador, Bartolome Mitre 1324, Ciudad Vieja
    A classic pub with occasional live music open seven days a week. Mainly pop, cumbia, reggaeton and bachata.
- Bluzz Bar, Canelones 760 esquina Ciudadela
    Small bar just around a busy corner from other good bars featuring good alternative and rock bands. Attracts a 20s-30s crowd.
    www.facebook.com/bluzzbar
- Clash City Rockers, Aquiles Lanza 1234, Centro
    Brit-rock themed bar with nicely grungy edge, pool and jukebox.
- Hendrix Music Bar, Lavalleja 1018 casi Rambla, Carrasco

Medium-size venues

The first three venues typically play host to shows featuring more alternative international acts and well-known Uruguayan bands.

- La Trastienda, Daniel Fernández Crespo 1763, Centro
- Montevideo Music Box (MMBox), Dámaso Antonio Larrañaga 3195 esq. Joanicó
- BJ Sala, Uruguay 960, Centro
- Sala Zitarrosa, 18 de julio 1012, Centro
    Classic concert venue run by the local government primarily featuring national bands of all genres. It's a former cinema so the acoustics are not great.
- Sala Zavala Muniz, in the Solis Theatre, Buenos Aires esq. Bartolomé Mitre, Ciudad Vieja
    Small theatre with first-world sound and lighting.
- Centro Cultural de España, Rincon 629, Ciudad Vieja
    Shows are usually free and early (around 7 pm). You are let in by order of arrival, so plan to arrive about 30 minutes before.
- SODRE Sala Auditorio Nelly Goitiño, 18 de Julio 930, Centro
    500-seater

Large venues featuring big national and international artists
- SODRE Auditorio Nacional Adela Reta, Andes esq Mercedes, Centro
    Montevideo's largest and newest theatre and world-class infrastructure including incredible acoustics. Hosts the national ballet, 2000-seater.

- Solis Theatre, Buenos Aires esq. Bartolomé Mitre
    Uruguay's oldest theatre, 900-seater.
- Teatro de Verano (Summer Theatre), Parque Rodo on the rambla
    The seat of the carnival competition. This 4,000-seater is open air and can be chilly in the evening as the breeze comes off the River Plate. Take a sweater!

How to find out what's on

As a musician I love to recommend off-the-beaten-path shows most days, mainly in Montevideo but following requests I am doing my best to cover great shows happening in the interior too. I post around midday on the Guru'Guay Facebook page.

Most clubs in Uruguay tend to use Facebook very actively and will list that night's show on their page. All these Facebook pages are public and you can access their info even if you are a die-hard Facebook-phobe.

For a pretty complete listing of shows plus venue addresses plus maps, check out the Yamp Agenda[38] [in Spanish]

Buying tickets and reserving tables

It's usually fine to roll up to most venues and get in, unless the band is super popular.

Tickets for medium and large venues are usually bought through **ticket agencies** like Abitab or the box office.

Most bars will charge you the *cubierto artistico* (cover charge all or a percentage of which goes to the artist) along with your drinks bill at the end of the night.

You can usually reserve a table through a locale's Facebook page. Write a message saying: *Por favor, reservame una mesa para x personas para el show de hoy. Gracias* (Please reserve me a table for x people for today's show. Thanks).

Show times and punctuality Be aware that most shows in small venues may start anything from 30 minutes to an hour later than advertised, unless the advertising states "punctual". Shows in large venues will start on time.

---

38 http://www.yamp.com.uy/agenda

Gay Montevideo

Uruguay is the most gay-friendly country in South America according to the Spartacus International Gay Guide. In Montevideo, it's common to see same-sex couples holding hands around town and on the rambla, the 25-kilometre promenade that borders the River Plate. And while some members of the older generation may be taking their time to come around to the changes, younger generations are openly supportive of their gay peers. The city is one of the few in the world to have a homo-monument.

Being such a small city, there are just a handful of gay bars and clubs, with most people opting to hang out with their friends wherever, regardless of sexual orientation.

Getting information

Friendly Point A tourist information centre for gay visitors. Head over to the Parque Rodó neighbourhood and talk to Carolina or Fernanda. They don't speak great English, but say "we'll make ourselves understood".
Salterain 931 almost on the corner of Gonzalo Ramirez street, Parque Rodó. Monday to Friday, 10 till 6.

Bars and night clubs

The gay scene in Montevideo is not huge so evening venues tend to open Wednesday to Sunday. Gay venues are welcoming of people of all stripes. There are several typical gay nightclubs – with names like Chains – just like those you can find in any other city. You might be anywhere in the world. So to check out REAL UruGAY, the Guru recommends:

Small Club

Brandzen 2172 bis on the corner of Acevedo Díaz, Cordón

A tiny pub cafe-concert type venue which is indeed tiny. Small's advertising banner is "The perfect previa" – the *previa* being the first course of the evening's action before moving on to the main dish. The *previa* at Small starts about 10 pm and the place will be packed by 11 pm as folks arrive for the show, which typically starts at 11 or 11.30 pm. There's no charge for the shows other than to buy a drink (known as *consumición*). Open Wednesday to Sunday from 10 pm.

Il Tempo

Gonzalo Ramirez 2121, Parque Rodó

Il Tempo is open Thursdays to Sundays (and Wednesdays during the warmer months) on a typical Uruguayan schedule. Saturday night is "ladies night" (not exclusively so). The action starts after midnight with an all-women show starting not earlier than 3 am and often at 4 am in the morning. Much of the clientele moves en masse from Small Club to Il Tempo. On Sundays there's a talent show. What makes it perhaps quintessentially UruGAY is that the talents are often accompanied by mums, dads and grandparents.

Celebrations and commemorations

Annual Diversity March – the last Friday of September

Uruguayans have an earnest approach to politics and social justice. So it feels in keeping to me that Montevideo's equivalent of Pride is called the Diversity March (Marcha por la Diversidad) and takes place in the mercilessly cold month of September (okay, I exaggerate, but you should be aware that September is winter here). The march starts at the Plaza de Independencia and ends on the steps of the Intendencia of Montevideo.

I remember joining the march around 2001 and we were a few hundred souls. Even 10 years ago, marchers numbered less than a thousand. However, the last decade has seen significant change. Uruguay became the first country in Latin America to pass marriage equality laws in 2013 and the 2015 march was the most numerous ever with an estimated 30,000 attendees from all walks of life. Perhaps, one commentator wrote, it won't be long now before Uruguay is ready for a celebration and "Pride".

Sexual Diversity Month – September

Every September, the Intendencia of Montevideo and the Ministry of Tourism promote a month-long sexual diversity agenda with events, talks, conferences and fairs. This being Uruguay, the programme will only likely be out at the end of August, or even the first days of September itself (sigh…).

Montevideo homomonument

In 2005, Montevideo became one of the few cities in the world to have a homo-monument – a rose-coloured granite statue in the shape of a triangle inscribed with the words: "To Honour Diversity is to Honour Life". The monument is tucked in a little plaza in the Old City of Montevideo. Beware that the plaza is in miserable shape and deserves a good make-over.

Plaza de la Diversidad Sexual, just off Bartolome Mitre street between Sarandi and Rincon, down a small street called Policia Vieja.

FOOD & DRINK

Food & Drink

What time do the locals eat?

And other culinary conundrums

Restaurant opening times in Uruguay are similar to those in Argentina. Breakfast and lunch at "normal" times and a very late dinner.

Restaurant opening times

Breakfast Around 9 am until about 11 am, though it is possible to find some restaurants in more commercial neighbourhoods like Ciudad Vieja and Centro opening from 7.30 am.

Lunch From 12 noon until 3 pm. To avoid waiting for a table arrive before 1 pm. Most restaurants stop serving by 3.30-4 pm.

Dinner From 8 pm till closing. Uruguayans typically go out for dinner at 9.30 or 10 pm. So you can get served from 8 pm but expect to be the only people in the place until 9.30 or 10pm when the locals start to arrive. Restaurants tend to close when the customers have left, unless otherwise stated. Closing hours in a popular restaurant mid-week may be about 1 am and later on weekends.

Reservations

Very few restaurants take reservations – perhaps because of the nation's infamous lack of punctuality. So if you want to get a table straight away at a popular place, get there by noon for lunch or 8 pm for dinner and problem solved.

What is "guarnición"?

When a sidedish is included with a meal the menu will usually state **"con guarnición"**.

Sides in Montevideo usually include *fritas* (fries), *puré* (mashed potatoes) or *mixta* (typically a lettuce, tomato and onion salad). Some places may also offer *papa al plomo* (baked potato) or *arroz* (rice). Not all dishes include a side. As sides are comparatively expensive and can bump up your overall bill significantly, it is worth checking.

The "cubierto"

What you're dying to ask: What is the *cubierto* which appears on the bill? It's a **cover charge** – supposedly to cover bread and other incidentals. Don't expect that if you refuse the bread it will necessarily come off your bill – but you can try!

The *cubierto* ranges in price depending on the type of establishment but is typically anything between 40 and 90 pesos per person, though at least one very expensive restaurant charges 200 pesos.

The price of the cubierto should be included in the menu. Some restaurants do not charge a cubierto, and will advertise outside as follows *"No cobramos cubierto"*.

Seating tip for solo travellers

And actually for couples too. Sit at the bar to eat. You'll feel less conspicuous, people will strike up conversations, and you'll usually get the best food too!

The secret to making it to 10 pm dinnertime

You may be surprised to hear, given the late dining hours, that the typical Montevideo work day is 9 am till 5 pm with just an hour break for lunch. So how can they eat dinner so late? Let me let you into a secret.

On their way home from work they'll typically stop off at a bakery or fancier *confiteria* (cake shop) to pick up something for their *merienda* (tea-time). This is typically *bizcochos* (savoury pastries) or *masitas* (sweet ones), which they'll then scarf down with mate or coffee. Then they'll take an hour-long nap. And then it's time for dinner!

When in Rome...

While you're in Montevideo, I'd definitely recommend you get into the same habit – **early evening snack, siesta, late dinner** – that way you can take advantage of all the shows and music, which also start 9 pm at the earliest and often much later.

10 foods you must try

Uruguayan cuisine is simple. The staple is meat with a mixed salad, simply cooked but very tasty.

Cattle are still grass-fed so if you don't usually eat red meat, you can feel good about doing it here. You'll find the fruit and vegetables are full of flavour.

Uruguayans are proud of their pastas and pizzas, but especially if you've ever been to Italy, they are nothing to write home about. The pasta is often fresh which is great, but typically they are offered with a choice between four sauces and that's it. The pizza... let me be brutally honest, wait till you are in Buenos Aires.

So what should you make sure you try while you are in Montevideo?

- **Chivito** Ask for: chee-VEE-toe
  Basically a huge steak sandwich layered with cheese, bacon, lettuce, tomato, olives, fried or hard-boiled egg and mayo. You can have it *"al plato"* i.e. without the bread. Curiously, *chivito* translates as baby goat, and a *chivito canadiense* is a *chivito* with ham. You can rest assured that no goats or Canadians were involved in their preparation.

- **Asado** Ask for: aa-SAA-do or TEE-ra de aa-SAA-do
  A cut of beef, and a way of grilling food, usually using firewood in Uruguay (vs coals in Argentina). Ordering an *asado* will get you a full steak meal, usually for two or more, which includes at least two cuts of beef, sausage, blood sausage – morcilla, which comes in sweet (*dulce*) or savoury (*salada*) versions – and sometimes chicken. If you want ribs, ask for *tira de asado*.

- **Pamplona**
  If you really want to look like a local, instead of ordering a tira, ask for a *pamplona*. Made of deboned chicken or pork, rolled and stuffed with cheese, ham, sweet pepper and sometimes olives, this originated on Uruguayan grills.

- **Morrón relleno** Ask for: moh-RONE ray-ZZHEN-oh
  If you find yourself in yet another parrilla, here's a vegetarian option which is often not on the menu. *Morrón relleno* is a roasted pepper stuffed with melted cheese and olives and ham. To order it without the ham, ask for "*Un morrón relleno sin jamón*". Ask for: moh-RON ray-ZZHEN-oh SEEN ha-MONE

- **Ñoquis** Ask for: nee-YOK-ees
  The Spanish spelling for the Italian *gnocchi*, this filling pasta meal was and is still traditionally served every 29th of the month, the day before payday, in homes and restaurants too. It's considered good (financial) luck to put some money under your plate before you start eating.

- **Dulce de leche** Ask for: DOOL-say day LEH-chay
  A creamy caramel sauce or filling that's popular all over Latin America. Uruguayans eat it on EVERYTHING.

- **Alfajor** Ask for: al-faa-WHORE
  A sweet South American sandwich made from two shortbread-style cookies filled with *dulce de leche* and covered in white or dark chocolate or powdered sugar. My British relatives go practically orgasmic for them.

- **Principe Humberto** Ask for: prEEN-see-pay oom-BARE-toe
  A uniquely Uruguayan dessert made of Marie biscuits, meringue, double cream, *dulce de leche* (of course) and virtually nothing else. However, the taste is out of this world. Look for it in supermarket freezers and get yourself a whole tub!

- **Chajá** Ask for: cha-HA
  Considered the most Uruguayan of all desserts, chajá was created in 1927 by a tea-shop owner in Paysandú, a city west of Montevideo. Made of sponge cake, meringue chips, cream and peaches, the original recipe remains a secret. Many restaurants stock chajá wrapped in its distinctive white wax-paper wrapping from the factory in Paysandú.

- **Torta frita**
  On any cold, rainy or overcast afternoon, stands selling tortas fritas magically mushroom on every street corner (see picture above). It's the ultimate comfort street food. The dough, which is like donut dough, is rolled into a roughly 8-inch disc and deep-fried till it puffs up. You can buy it as it comes or ask for it to be sprinkled with sugar.

Wine

With more than 200 wineries – 80% within a 30-mile (50 km) radius of Montevideo – Uruguay is the new world's undiscovered wine jewel.

Some vineyards are over a hundred years old; many of the newer ones are owned by foreigners who have fallen in love with Uruguay, like Leslie Fellows from California, one of the owners of all-women-run estate winery Artesana.

It was typical for families, many of whom descend from Italians and Spaniards, to grow grapes and make their own wine at home. I have a relative whose family have a tub to tread the grapes at home that dates from several generations ago.

Since 2000, wine-making has been professionalised under the tutelage of renowned flying wine-makers coinciding with a new generation of local enologists getting their wine-making credentials in Uruguay and specialising abroad. These young wine-makers are daredevils, making new styles, trying new blends and all importantly getting great results.

For years, but most noticeably in the last decade, wines from Uruguay are winning gold and silver medals in international competitions.

There are now hundreds of labels, and every month you can get to try new and better wines. I have been lucky enough to have the expert opinions of wine experts Viviana del Rio and Claudio Angelotti from Bodegas del Uruguay, the only website exclusively dedicated to promoting Uruguayan wines.

20 of the best Uruguayan wines

I asked Viviana and Claudio to select 20 of the best that you must not miss. They agonised and came up with this list which includes wines for all tastes and pockets.

Alto de la Ballena Tannat Viognier
Antigua Bodega Stagnari Osiris Merlot
Artesana Tannat Zinfandel Merlot
Bertolini & Broglio Exotic Tannat Ultra Premium
Bouza Albariño
Bouza Cocó Chardonnay Albariño
Bouza Monte Vide Eu (blend)
Campotinto Tannat
Familia Deicas Atlántico Sur Single Vineyard El Carmen (blend)
Familia Deicas Massimo Deicas Tannat
Garzón Pinot Noir Rosé
Garzón Viognier
Giménez Méndez Alta Reserva Sauvignon Blanc
H. Stagnari Chardonnay de Virginia
Irurtia Grappa Gewürztraminer
Irurtia Km. 0 Río de la Plata Gran Reserva Pinot Noir
J. Chiappella Unum (blend)
Marichal Reserve Collection Pinot Noir Blanc de Noir - Chardonnay
Montes Toscanini Corte Supremo (blend)
Viña Varela Zarranz Guidaí Detí Gran Reserva Tannat

12 of the best budget wines

Claudio and Viviana have done it again! Here are their top picks for people like my folks who like wine but don't want to pay an arm and a leg. Again, organised alphabetically. Being a beer woman myself, I've included the descriptions as provided by our experts.

You can expect to pay between **190 and 250 Uruguayan pesos (currently 6-8 USD)** for a good quality budget wine. This is more expensive than wines from Argentina and Chile and one of the drawbacks of the family-run model of local vineyards in Uruguay. Small wineries have high production costs.

The good news is that you will be able to taste some varieties which are quite unusual, starting from the signature grape Tannat to many of European origin coming from Portugal, France, Spain and Italy.

Reds

- **Artesana Zinfandel** The only winery in Uruguay making this variety of red – with great succes.
- **Castillo Viejo Catamayor Reserva de la Familia Pinot Noir** A classic red from the Etcheverry family, very delicate aromas and brightness.
- **Giménez Méndez 100 Años Alta Reserva Tannat** Uruguay's signature grape in its best expression in this price range.
- **Montes Toscanini Carlos Montes Crianza Merlot** Delicate black fruit notes in the nose and a round and long finish
- **Varela Zarranz Tannat Roble** Sample how Uruguay's most well-known red benefits from well managed oak so that the wine retains its fruity notes.

Whites

- **Filgueira Sauvignon Gris** The only local producers of this very good white.
- **H. Stagnari Selección La Puebla Gewürztraminer** A variety that has found in this country a balanced climate to develop flowers and white fruit.
- **Irurtia Km. 0 Río de la Plata Gran Reserva Viognier** One of the largest wineries located in Carmelo offers this jewel to enjoy in aromas and taste.
- **Los Cerros de San Juan Lahusen Riesling** From its Colonia terroir close to the coasts of the Uruguay River, where these grapes ripen to their best expression.
- **Pisano Verde Virgen** This white blend is unique for its pétillance (slightly sparkling). A great find among the white wines in which Uruguay excels.
- **Pizzorno Don Próspero Sauvignon Blanc** Carefully balanced in its deep tropical fruit aroma and acidity, this variety is a great achievement for Uruguay.

Rosé

- **Establecimiento Juanicó Don Pascual Blanc de Noirs** A rosé wine that matches every possible pairing with elegance.

Craft beer

The beer market in Uruguay is captured by mass-produced beers all produced by the same now Brazilian-owned brewery. They include Patricia, Pilsen and a few places sell the ridiculously cheap Norteña. The "green bottles" – that's Zillertal and Stella Artois – are considered the "posh" beers. Personally, I find Stella is the only mass-produced beer that is genuinely palatable.

So go for the good stuff. Go for craft beer. More and more restaurants and bars are realising that this is what clients want, so check on the menu to see what's available. The number of craft breweries in Uruguay has exploded over recent years – now standing at 21.

Here are some you can check out when you are in Montevideo.

- **Montevideo Brew House** A small brewery with restaurant in the leafy streets of "inland" Pocitos. They produce anything from six beers and you can request a taster tray of six of the most popular before you move on to pints. Great dry stout, especially if you are dreaming of a cool Guinness. See *Restaurants*
- **Davok** Consistent medal winners at the South Beer Cup, their wonderful brews are sold at MBH. They also share the same brew master.
- **Birra Bizarra** One of the best ales you are likely to run across in Montevideo and one of the best designed products anywhere in the world. The Indian Pale Ale is outstanding and the Blonde Ale perfect for a day at the beach.
- **El Leon de Aiguá** Lovely creamy blonde beer from a tiny brewery in the hills of Lavalleja.
- **Chela Brandon** The first Uruguayan beer to obtain kosher certification!
- **Cabesas Bier** They produce Uruguay's most internationally successful beers and are based in inland Tacuarembó.
- **Volcánica** Brewed in Las Toscas, a small beach town in Canelones about 50 kilometres from Montevideo.
- **Dharma** The second best consumable to come out of legendary Fray Bentos, Dharma is produced by Uruguay's only female brewmaster.
- **Mastra** One of the earliest craft brewers and now the biggest. Likely because of their commercial aspirations (and good for them) I find their beers too tuned to the South American palate (ie too sweet) and unfortunately not to mine. They have a stand in the Montevideo Agricultural Market.

Restaurants

Uruguayans like their food plain and simple, and most like it meaty. Give them a well-cooked piece of beef and a *"mixta"* and they are happy.

Visitors to Uruguay have often been to Argentina before they get here, and I think it's fair to say many of you maybe somewhat tired of meat. So... while I touch on *parrillas* – the local term for grill restaurants – I'm going to focus on options for people who may be just a little bit *cansado de carne*[39] and looking for veggies, fish or gourmet.

I think it's about right to say that the best place for gourmet food in Montevideo is the Ciudad Vieja. A number of small restaurants are serving top-notch food at great prices, serving the local business crowd. This means that most are only open at lunch-time, so if you are a foodie you will want to make sure you put this in your itinerary.

Note I give opening days and times as a *guide*. If visiting a particular establishment is a matter of life or death for you I recommend you contact them in advance. Beware that a number of the smaller restaurants may not take credit cards. I've marked where I know that they don't but again, always have some cash with you, just in case.

---

39 Fed up of meat

Lunch and evenings

Dueto, Bartolome Mitre 1386 between Sarandi and Rincon, Ciudad Vieja
Run by its owners Mercedes (front of house) and Pablo (the chef). Their set menu is great value with three courses including a drink for about 700 pesos. Good-size portions, extremely fresh fish. The art-deco building is an ex-police station and the bathrooms are located where the cells were.
Mon-Sat 12-3.30 pm and dinner from 8 pm.

Candy Bar, on the corner of Durazno and Santiago de Chile, Palermo
Retro bar with food inspired by Argentine chef Hernan's grandmother's home cooking. The menu is deliberately short (four main dishes and tapas) and the food is tip-top quality. Prices are very reasonable and portions of the tapas a good size. Candy Bar serves wine by Artesana and craft beer by Volcánica. There are a few outdoor tables on the street but you may want to stay indoors to listen to the great music selection. I've had guests ask for a copy of the playlist before they leave!
Tue-Fri 11 am-3 pm and 7 pm-closing (around 1 am), Sat 12 noon-4 pm and 8 pm-closing, Sun brunch 12-4 pm, tapas till 6 pm. No credit cards.

Foc, Ramon Fernández 285, Punta Carretas
Before you ask, Foc means fire in Catalán – chef Martin Lavecchia trained at Michelin-starred restaurants south of Barcelona. Outstanding Spanish-influenced cuisine with fast and notably friendly service. Superb fish and mmm... the desserts... You can see that there's a good, respect-filled vibe in the kitchen and Martin is out chatting to customers and even cleaning tables. Foc's previous incarnation in the Ciudad Vieja was notable for its excellent prices – I hope it stays that way. Foc opens in Punta Carretas from February 10 2016.
Tue-Sat 8-11.30 pm or midnight

La Fonda, Perez Castellano 1422 between Washington and 25 de Mayo, Ciudad Vieja
Quirky little restaurant which is changing the face of the Old City where they are located. Their vegan chef cooks only what has been bought that day. They use only organic vegetables and make their own pasta. On weekends they offer local lamb. Live music on Thursdays. Some outdoor seating on the pedestrian street.
Tue-Sun 11 am-6 pm, Thurs-Sat evenings from 8pm.

Montevideo Brew House, Libertad 2592 esq. Viejo Pancho, Pocitos
MBH is a craft brewery which opened a restaurant to pay the bills. So they take their beer production very seriously but their food is also pretty good – especially the ojo de bife (tenderest steak) and the spicy home-made fried potatoes. Regarding the beer, MBH stock their own beer and the excellent Davok (love their IPA). The MBH dry stout rivals Guinness. Order their beer sampler to find out which you like most.
Mon-Wed 5 pm-2 am, Thurs-Sat 5 pm-3 am. Closed Sundays.

La Perdiz, Guipuzcoa 350 esq. Baliñas, Punta Carretas

This grill, just down from the Punta Carretas shopping mall, gets rightly packed out so reserve the day before or go at opening time, 7.30 pm. Their menu is very complete and includes *parrilla* and Basque cuisine as well as fish and seafood. Excellent rack of lamb. They have been kind enough to let guests of mine watch international sports events on their TV until way past midnight.
Open every day 12-4 pm and dinner from 7.30 pm

Café Bacacay, Buenos Aires opposite the Solis Theatre, Cuidad Vieja

This classic Montevideo cafe-bar is popular with the theatre crowd, and for those staying in the Old City it could turn into your local. Food is served all day. Good fish. Good sandwiches (check out the capresse). Cheesecake to die for. Cocktails. Mon-Fri 9 am-1 am, Sat 10 am-1 am.

Santa Catalina, Ciudadela esquina Canelones, on the border between Ciudad Vieja and Centro

You won't get a bigger, tastier meal for less in Montevideo than in this spit-and-sawdust cantina which is usually crowded with young people. Pepe Mujica, Uruguay's infamously "rustic" ex-president came here for lunch on his first day in office. Try the oven-roasted *ternera* (chunk of veal) or *asado* (ribs) or the *canelones* pasta which is big enough for two. If the meat comes in a pool of fat and juices, it's because they expect you to mop it up with bread as a treat. I know, I know. Remedy the situation by asking for an extra plate. Great place to watch the sun go down over an ice-cold beer. They tell me they open every day except Sundays but my experience is that they can close on a whim and sometimes for an entire month at a time, such as they close all January. Open from midday till late. No credit cards.

Lunchtime only

Estrecho, Sarandi 460, Ciudad Vieja

OMG the BEST food, prepared right in front of you by a virtually all-female team led by French chef

Benedicte Buffard. The menu is always varied and Benedicte uses the the best ingredients. The service is outstanding. Prices are much below what you would expect to pay elsewhere for the presentation and quality. You eat at the bar so good for two people but not more – unless you are JUST there for the food. And why not?

Mon-Fri lunchtime. No credit cards.

La Pasionaria, Reconquista 587, Ciudad Vieja

Craving veggies? This lunchtime restaurant serves more creative food than the usual Uruguayan steak, including vegetarian dishes and good home-made soups. It is located in a gift shop and gallery specialising in unusual gifts by designers and craftspeople in a lovely, colonial building with a central courtyard.

Mon-Sat lunch.

Urbani, Plaza Zabala, Ciudad Vieja

Run by Quebecois chef Gabriel, Urbani offers breakfasts, brunches and great value lunches with a glass of wine starting at 10 USD. It is one of the few places in Montevideo to offer home-made french fries. That alone warrants a mention! With a charming view of Plaza Zabala.

Mon-Fri 9-5 pm.

Sin Pretensiones, Sarandí 366, Ciudad Vieja

Comfort food cooked exquisitely in a vintage furniture store where the 20s oak table you're sitting at is up for sale. A family concern, led by chef Guillermina, they've run gastronomy businesses in Patagonian ski resorts, glitzy Punta del Este, estancias and it shows. Original and with an attention to detail that is unusual in relaxed Montevideo.

Mon-Fri 9.30am-6.30pm

Bodega Bouza (Bouza Vineyard), 13.5 kilometres from the centre of Montevideo

Eighty percent of Uruguay's vineyards are within a 30 mile radius of Montevideo and Bouza is 12-15 minutes from downtown by cab! A French oak-barrel seller stayed at our guesthouse for a week and visited 17 wine-makers. At the end of her stay, we asked her to recommend the best vineyard and she chose Bodega Bouza, which offers bilingual tours and has a truly excellent restaurant. You can also do wine-tasting. They have a standard range and a premium range. Check the Bouza website and book your tour before you go. As Uruguay has a zero-tolerance policy on drinking and driving, go by cab. The cost is around 450 pesos one way to go to Bouza from the Old City. Bouza will call a cab for you on your return. Say: *BOW-za*, as in bow-tie

Open lunch-time almost every day of the year.

And let's finish with the biggest meat fest of them all..

Mercado del Puerto, Ciudad Vieja

The Guardian described this place as "Disneyland for carnivores". I've not seen any place like it, not even in Argentina. Flames everywhere! It's a bit of a tourist trap and more expensive than most parrillas, but saying that, Uruguayans love it too! So it's really not to be missed. Vegetarians or those who would like the experience but want to order something lighter and then have lunch elsewhere should order the classic roasted stuffed pepper with melted cheese and olives and ham, which is often not on the menu. To get it without the ham, order "*Un morrón relleno sin jamón*". Open every lunch-time (12-4 pm) – weekends are the liveliest.

Breakfast

Breakfast is traditionally not big in Uruguay. A typical breakfast is a *café con leche* with a couple of *bizcochos* (sweet or savoury pastries) or a *sandwiche caliente* (toasted ham and cheese or tomato and cheese sandwich).

So why am I doing a separate restaurant section on breakfast? Because I love breakfast and finally Montevideo is starting to get some decent breakfast options. So I'm hoping Guru'Guay can give them a good boost.

As ever, opening and closing times may be "flexible". Also see *Historic cafes and bars*

Urbani, Plaza Zabala, Ciudad Vieja
For breakfast lovers, Quebecois chef Gabriel offers mid-week breakfasts and brunches overlooking the charming Plaza Zabala in the Old City. Breakfast includes four versions of Eggs Benedict and authentic French omelet with goat's cheese. The fresh fruit side dish when we went was unexpectedly packed with kiwi and strawberries.
Mon-Fri from 9 am

Café Brasilero, Ituzaingo 1447, Ciudad Vieja
Founded in 1877, with its wood-panelled walls, hat stands and gas lamps, Cafe Brasilero is a great little historic cafe frequented by Montevideo's literati. The coffee is great and it's perfect to sit by the huge open windows and watch the world go by. Newspapers and Wi-Fi provided.
Mon-Sat from 9 am

Clube Brasileiro, 18 de Julio 994, Centro

Take the elevator up and step back in time at this 100-year-old social club with stained glass windows, art-deco mosaic floors, a billiard table, fireplaces. They serve fresh fruit smoothies (*licuados*, though the menu says "jugos" erroneously) as well as the typical Uruguayan breakfast options.
Mon-Sat from 8 am

Café Las Misiones, 25 de Mayo 449, Ciudad Vieja

The building where Las Misiones is located was originally a pharmacy built in 1907. The emblematic green antique-tiled frontage survives intact to this day. Inside the feel is vintage and there's an enormous stained glass ceiling.
Mon-Fri from 7.30 am

Café Bacacay, opposite the Solis Theatre, Ciudad Vieja

The Bacacay is a Montevidean classic, popular with the theatre and arts crowd. It's great to visit any time of day but is a very civilised way to start the day with a classic Uruguayan breakfasts and newspapers. There is outdoor seating surrounded by planters opposite the Solis Theatre so good for people watching.
Mon-Fri from 9 am, Sat from 10 am

Sundays

Candy Bar, on the corner of Durazno and Santiago de Chile, Palermo

For Sunday brunch lovers, Candy Bar's set brunch is not to be missed. The superb brunch includes Hernan's twice-cooked fragrant scrambled eggs with capresse toast, French toast with fruit and a honey dressing, plus juice and great coffee. Some outdoor seating and wonderful music selection.
Sunday 12-4 pm

Any cafe on Tristan Narvaja street, Centro

Breakfast on a Sunday in Montevideo is a challenge. I usually recommend that my guests check out the Tristan Narvaja market which is only held on Sundays. Head to Tristan Narvaja street and pick one of the numerous spit-and-sawdust cafes that line the street. Order a *cafe y medialunas* (coffee and croissants) and watch the locals go about their business. Wander the market side-streets and then head over to Candy Bar for brunch or the Port Market for a majorly meaty lunch.

Restaurants for wine-lovers

Unfortunately, despite the fact that Uruguayan wines are prized internationally, the market is flooded with low-priced imported wines mainly from Argentina and Chile. So the average Montevidean restaurant has a short wine list with few local options.

However, there are several restaurants in Montevideo with excellent sommeliers and several with wine cellars. So, if you are serious about wine, here's where to go.

El Palenque, Port Market, Ciudad Vieja
One of the classic Mercado del Puerto restaurants, El Palenque stocks a large number of wine labels in its cellar and offers sommelier service.

Francis (two locations, Punta Carretas and Carrasco)
Although expensive, it keeps its reputation as one of the best in the city where sommelier service is offered.

La Casa Violeta, Rambla Armenia 3667, Buceo
A beautiful view of the Port of Buceo and advice on wines from Somm. Alejandro Cortinas.

Museo del Vino, Maldonado 1150, Barrio Sur
A little wine bar with excellent live music which offers Uruguayan wine only, selected by the owner, Somm. Miguel Etchandy. Open Wed-Sat.

My Wine Bar, Benito Blanco 674, Pocitos
The only wine-themed hotel in Montevideo, the MySuites Hotel restaurant has a limited food menu and a long wine list. Wine is served by Somm. Mauricio Giménez with tastings six nights a week.

Panini's, 26 de Marzo 3586 at the World Trade Center, Pocitos
Another restaurant whose wine cellar has won No.1 place for many years running.

Rara Avis, in the Solís Theatre, Ciudad Vieja
Up-scale restaurant with one of the most complete wine cellars in all Montevideo.

Sacramento, Williman 594, Punta Carretas
Sacramento has been in business for more than 15 years with consistently good reviews. It offers a sommelier service.

1921 Restaurant, Sofitel Montevideo Hotel, Carrasco
Wines under the supervision of Uruguay's No.1 Sommelier, Federico De Moura, who gets wonderful reviews by customers. Federico represents Uruguay in international sommelierie contests.

SOCIETY & CULTURE

Society & Culture

Why is Uruguay like it is?

Some historical facts to get your head around Uruguay

With help from crack Uruguayan historian Aldo Marchesi, the Guru has answers to some of the questions you may have after you've wandered around Montevideo for a while.

Looking at Montevideo's magnificent architecture, Uruguay was once rich. What happened?

From the late 19th century to the 1950s, Montevideo was the capital of a very prosperous country whose wealth was based on exports of beef, leather and wool. It got rich selling primary materials to countries in Europe and elsewhere that were growing. Montevideo was very much part of the modern world with international theatre and dance troupes including Montevideo and Buenos Aires on their world-wide tours. The crisis came in the 1960s as the prices of raw material exports collapsed.

When the Old City WAS Montevideo

Montevideo was founded in 1726 by the Spanish as an exceptionally deep port on the banks of the River Plate. It was an entirely walled city. The walls were torn down in 1829 and nowadays only the Ciudadela, the arch which marks the entrance to the Sarandi pedestrian street, remains. Today the

Old City is the heart of government, finance and import and export so it's bustling during the week and much quieter on weekends. But years ago the Old City WAS Montevideo and for that reason it is still one of the only socio-economically mixed neighbourhoods in Montevideo, where rich rub shoulders with the poor, and for that reason one of the most interesting even nowadays.

Did Uruguay have a dictatorship like Chile and Argentina?

There was a dictatorship in Uruguay from 1973 to 1986. As prices for beef, etc. collapsed, inflation spiralled and the Uruguayan quality of life, which had been very high, fell. Students, the trade unions and an armed guerrilla protested the situation in the late 60s. Powerful sectors of society – the landowners, industrialists and some bankers – were of a conservative mind-set and there was a gradual move towards an authoritarian response which began with the prohibition of rival political parties and free media and culminated in the sitting president carrying out a kind of self-coup by dissolving parliament and banning all political parties, with the backing of sectors of the military. (Some military leaders were against the dictatorship and were jailed themselves. One general, Liber Seregni, went on to found the Frente Amplio, the progressive coalition that has run the country since 2005).

Is it true that Uruguay's last president was a member of the guerrilla?

Pepe Mujica was a guerilla in the Tupamaros, a left-wing urban guerrilla group which styled themselves on Robin Hood. They aimed at keeping violence to a minimum and carrying out actions that denounced the elite rather than terrorising the population. For example, they robbed and exhibited accounting ledgers to demonstrate the hold of banks over politicians. However, the idyll ended with the assassination of a US official in a story retold in the Costa-Gavros movie *State of Seige*. Pepe was arrested and jailed for 13 years, two years of which he was held at the bottom of a dry well. When democracy returned he joined the current governing coalition, the Frente Amplio, and became infamous as the senator who arrived to Congress on a tatty Vespa. He became president in 2005 in a ceremony which included his reviewing of the very same brigade that had imprisoned him so many years previously. When his term ended, a huge gathering (pictured above) formed outside the presidential buildings spontaneously to see him off at 6pm on his last day.

Where is Uruguay's indigenous population?

Uruguayans have been traditionally taught that Uruguay was the only country in Latin America with no indigenous people. The myth was that most Uruguayans were the descendants of immigrants from Spain and Italy along with a tiny percentage of African descendants and that the indigenous people were run off the land. However, the Uruguayan genome was mapped several years ago and demonstrates that practically all Uruguayans have a mix of European, African and indigenous genes. In fact, 30% are born with the "Mongolian Spot" at the base of their spine, a genetic marker shared by Latin American indigenous people throughout the continent.

And it seems to me that Uruguayans' First Nations past is evident in their passion for mate drinking, the traditional widespread sale of herbal remedies and the continuing popularity of indigenous names like Tabaré and Yamandú. The current president is called Tabaré Vazquez.

How come a little country like Uruguay did something as radical as legalise cannabis?

It's actually legal to smoke and possess marijuana in a lot of countries, what is different about Uruguay's legislation is that for the first time a national government is taking charge of the entire supply chain – from crop to distribution. But what looks like an audacious political policy is not so surprising in Uruguay[40].

In 1931, to ensure that citizens didn't kill themselves drinking unregulated moonshine, the government created ANCAP, the government-run industry which today still refines oil, makes cement – and produces whisky. It's part of a long and pragmatic tradition of market intervention and nationalisation. The state controls all public utilities and fixes prices for essentials like milk. Uruguay was the fourth country in the world to ban smoking in public places and has pioneered some of the tightest controls on tobacco in the world. With marijuana, the government is planning for a high-quality, legal product to be sold in a safe environment at a price that competes with that offered by illegal dealers.

Can I drink the water?

Uruguay is the only country in Latin America which provides virtually universal access to fresh drinking water. So yes, you can drink the water virtually anywhere. Public services in general here are very good – and they are all in state-controlled hands. In the 1990s there was a huge wave of privatisation of services across Latin America, promoted by the World Bank and the IMF. The neo-liberal government that was in power in Uruguay at the time attempted to privatise a bunch of utilities and was forced to call a referendum on the decision, with 68% of the population voting to keep utilities nationalised. Water, electricity, gas and fixed telephony are still all controlled by state monopoly. You can buy a mobile telephone from a number of providers, but the most popular continues to be the state-run ANTEL. Oh, and Montevideo's sanitation system was the first in Latin America (so you can throw toilet paper down the toilet – unlike so many other countries!)

---

40 http://guruguay.com/about-uruguay/

How come drumming is such a big part of Montevideo culture?

Anyone who spends enough time strolling around Montevideo will run into comparsas (drumming troupes) on the street. Every neighbourhood has its comparsas, and the candombe rhythms they play are named after streets in the Barrio Sur neighbourhood – the former slave district of Montevideo. Montevideo was a major slave-trade port as was Buenos Aires. The first African slaves arrived in 1750, and large numbers of Africans were trafficked here for the next 60 years by the English and the Spanish. While their culture was repressed by the Spanish, the Africans who stayed in Montevideo communicated with each other through drumming and this has become a major part of Montevideo popular culture, influencing music and dance. Slavery was abolished in 1846 and when men (not women) received the vote, all men regardless of race were enfranchised. While the black population of Argentina was decimated in the 1800s by disease and war, in the last census in 2011, almost one in ten Uruguayans recognised themselves to be *afro-descendientes*. The Llamadas, or drumming calls, are the most exciting part of carnival in Montevideo today.

Why is Uruguay so progressive?

I would say that most Uruguayans have an intrinsic belief in equality and hold that an egalitarian society needs a social security net. Even the traditional conservative political parties would be considered socialist elsewhere. This philosophy is the legacy of a free-thinking president called Jose Batlle y Ordoñez (Batlle is pronounced *BY-zhay*). Batlle inspired a movement which lasted from 1904 until the early 1930s (after his death) which promoted concerted state action to improve society.

Waves of immigrants from Spain and Italy arrived from the 1870s onwards and new and old citizens felt very strongly that in Uruguay they were creating something new, free from the fetters of tradition. They were building a modern society. They pioneered free compulsory public education from the 1870s including for women (the university system is still free today).

Batlle, who was a journalist and part of a wealthy political family, like many of the elite at the time shared this belief and as a consequence rejected the church. He lived in sin with his partner instead of marrying and gleefully organised huge outdoor *asados* over Easter rather than going to mass. And Batlle was very much part of his generation. At the turn of the century a group of intellectuals, the Generation of 900, including feminist writer Delmira Agustini, were at the modernist vanguard celebrating libertarian values and eccentricity, including sexual freedom and drug experimentation.

Seeing the problems that Europe had as a result of the unfettered excesses of the Industrial Revolution, Batlle said, let's learn from this, let's have progress but let it be more harmonious for the workers. Private monopolies were turned taken over by the government. The government brought in unemployment compensation (1914) and the eight-hour workday (1915). Battle himself welcomed anarchists (the "terrorists" of the day) fleeing Europe, as long as they came pacifically, and he asked them to train workers regarding their rights.

He backed universal suffrage regardless of sex and race. When white men got the vote, so did black men. And women had the vote (1917) long before they did in many European countries.

During his terms in office, religious instruction in public schools was banned and a complete separation of church and state[41] was written into the 1917 Constitution. A couple of years later, all religious holidays were secularised, explaining why Easter Week is known as Tourism Week here. If you are wondering why there is a huge cross near the Tres Cruces bus station, this is because current president Tabaré Vazquez, then Mayor of Montevideo, authorised the cross for the arrival of Pope John Paul II. Many Montevideans are still annoyed by this.

Besides separation of church and state, divorce was legalised in 1907 (compare with neighbours Argentina and Chile which did not legalise until 1987 and 2004 respectively!) and even abortion was legalised in the 1930s for a brief period until doctors wrested control back from midwives.

---

41 http://guruguay.com/why-uruguayans-celebrate-tourism-week-not-easter/

The Uruguayan character

It's dangerous to generalise, right? But let me entertain you with a few entirely personal anecdotes which I believe illustrate something of the Uruguayan character.

Super friendly people

"Perhaps Montevideo's best assets are its 25 kilometres of promenade waterfront and its exceptionally friendly people. That friendliness is exhibited over and over again – the woman who crossed the street to explain that the restaurant I thought was closed would be opening in 15 minutes, the museum staff who allowed me to come in to the buildings to take pictures, the elderly waiter in a Pocitos cafe who put the wi-fi password into my phone for me despite us not having a language in common and the assistant at La Pasionaria who happily explained many of the design items to me without applying any obvious pressure to buy. Very refreshing after a week in beautiful but frenetic Buenos Aires." – by my guest Adrian Yekkes of London, posted in his architecture blog

Uruguayan presidents (and other celebs) are down-to-earth, like the people they serve

Mechanic Gerhald Acosta was hitching a ride home from his work place in western Uruguay. Acosta had been on the roadside for over an hour, ignored by the drivers of 30 or so cars, when a car with official licence plates followed by a regular car pulled up. A man got out of the second car and offered him a ride in the car in front – the one with the official plates. "When I got in, I thought to myself – I know that woman," said Acosta. It was Lucia Topolansky, senator and First Lady, sitting in the back of the car with Manuela, infamous three-legged First Mutt. And President Pepe Mujica was in the front seat. This story hit the headlines internationally in January 2015. The source was the mechanic himself, who had posted photos of Lucia and Pepe on his Facebook page.

The current president of Uruguay, Tabaré Vazquez, is a doctor. In October 2015, he saved the life of a teenager who was suffering a severe allergic reaction on a flight. It was the third time Vazquez had stepped in to give medical assistance on a plane. Uruguayan presidents fly on commercial airlines of course. And Mujica insisted on flying coach.

Ruben Rada is a much-loved musician whose long career has had a huge impact on contemporary Uruguayan music. His daughter went to the same school as our son, and he would regularly come and pick her up at the same time as we'd go and pick up our son. All the kids would be hanging off of him or would shout out his name. He never looked bothered.

Courteous – At your orders

Uruguayans are very polite. In fact I often think of them as the British of Latin America. They have s a certain reserve, that is unexpected in a Latin American, though then when you have a Uruguayan as a friend, they are very warm and affectionate and will really go out of their way for you. But as a stranger, in the street – besides a couple of circumstances that I will venture into in next year's guide! – in general you will be treated very courteously.

One expression sums this courtesy up for me. If you admire something someone owns, the Uruguayan auto-response is "A las órdenes", as in, "at your service" or "it's all yours". It's such a habit that people even extend their generosity to completely inappropriate items that could never ever be lent or given to another person. Once I was admiring a friend's glasses. "A las órdenes" he said to me, and it was only after I fell around laughing that he realised that what he had said was kind of absurd. The glasses were prescription only. I still find the expression charming, though.

Even the robbers can be amiable

My friend Analia had been having a particularly bad day, when to top it all off a mugger jumped out in front of her, made as if he had a gun in his pocket, and shouted, "Flaca, dame la plata!" (Skinny chick, give me your purse). It was the final straw. "Ay, noooo!!" wailed Ani. Hearing her tone of sheer frustration, the would-be mugger's face was overcome with concern. He pulled his hands out of his pockets to show they were really empty, and then backed away keeping his hands up. "I was only joking! Really, it was just a joke," he insisted until he had backed around the corner and disappeared.

Vito, another friend of mine, was coming out of work and it was pay day. She had the bad luck to run into a thief who blocked her path and demanded cash. There was no way that she was going to give this guy her hard-earned salary. Standing her ground she looked him straight in the eye and said, "OK, I'm going to give you some money. But NOT if you speak to me in that tone." The mugger was completely taken aback and stopped dead. Thinking fast because she didn't want him to see how much money she really had on her, Vito commanded, "OK, stand back! If you want some money, you'll have to move away from me!" The guy backed away as Vito rummaged in her purse. Taking out a 20-peso note (about a dollar at the time) with great ceremony she sternly repeated "OK, I'm going to give you this. But you do NOT talk me like that ever again. Is that clear?" Her assailant apologised for having been a nuisance, thanked her profusely, turned on his heel and meekly walked away.

How to spot a Uruguayan anywhere in the world

It's easy. They will be carrying a gourd full of a dangerously hot herbal infusion that they sip through a metal straw and top up constantly from a thermos flask wedged under their shoulder – as they walk along. This drink is mate, a caffeine-based type of tea. And while Argentinians, Paraguayans and people from southern Brazil also drink mate, Uruguayans are the only ones that walk around serving their mates as they go (Argentinians will sit down and get the mate out). In fact there are signs on the buses here prohibiting mate consumption as you travel. Imagine what could happen at a sharp stop.

Proximity to Brazil

When I arrived in Uruguay I was amazed by how comfortable Uruguayans are with their biggest neighbour's language and culture. Everyone seemed to be able to throw around simple phrases and there is actually a language known as Portunhol which is spoken on the Brazilian-Uruguayan border which mixes the two languages. Uruguayan popular culture has adopted some expressions that come from Portuguese. For instance, in Brazil, if something is really great people say "Demais!" Uruguayans say "De más!" You would never hear this expression in Argentina.

"I love the smell of marijuana in the morning"

Marijuana was legalised in December 2013 and that first week after the law passed, there was a kind of crazy sentiment in the air – in a good, liberating way. I played a gig organised at a private house and the improvised bar advertised "happy cookies" on the menu. Someone recounted seeing a guy in our favourite hole-in-the-wall cantina in the Old City who sat down, ordered his beer and tossed a large zip-lock bag of fresh buds onto the table in full view. Then life settled back to usual.

Then come March, whenever I went to open my front door at home in Parque Rodó, there was a very strong smell of pot. The smell was so strong that I would stick my head out of the door and look left and right to see who the hell was smoking such a huge joint. But the street would be deserted. So I'd go back inside, scratching my head. This happened each time I opened the door over the next few days. THEN I realised – we have one of Montevideo's 40 growing co-ops directly across from our house. They grow on the roof. And it was harvest time.

Uruguayan expressions you won't hear anywhere else

The people living on either side of the River Plate share a similar accent and you can be forgiven for thinking that they sound exactly the same. They pronounce the double "ll" and "y" like zzhh, so "uruguayo" (Uruguayan) is pronounced oo-roo-GW-EYE-zzhoh, not oo-roo-GW-EYE-yo like it would be in most of Latin America. To the rest of Latin America, this sounds kind of sexy.

But the use of some particular words and expressions is a dead give-away that you are speaking to a Uruguayan as opposed to an Argentinian. Here's some for you to look out for.

Ta
Used in the same myriad ways an English-speaker uses "OK". It is a shortened form of the word "está" meaning "it is". Uruguayans pepper it throughout their speech.

Bo
Roughly translates as man or mate and is used similarly. It is the shortened form of "botija" which is a slang word for kid or kiddo. Uruguayans also use "che", but Argentinians never use "bo". Here you may hear the double-barrelled "che, bo!", like hey, man!

Todo bien
Roughly transates as "it's cool" or "don't stress". Typically used with bo and che! As in "Che, bo, todo bien!" It's an ultra-flexible phrase Uruguayans use to shrug off an annoying or depressing situation like water rolling off a duck's back. Its ubiquity illustrates their unruffled demeanour.

Vamo' arriba!
Plays a similar role to "todo bien" and the two are often used consecutively. Someone did something to piss you off but you are going to let it go? Uruguayans say: Todo bien bo, vamo' arriba. Can also be used to give someone encouragement.

Divino el dia!
I was in Buenos Aires recently and declared "Divino el dia!" or "Lovely day!" The Uruguayan with me gasped, you can tell you've been living in Montevideo for years, no one in Buenos Aires would ever use that expression!

Bárbaro!
Express your enthusiasm using this expression which translates as Fantastic!

Chau! Que pases bien!

"Chau" is the spelling used here for "Ciao", and "Que pases bien!" translates as "Have a good one!" This is a typical farewell demonstrating that Uruguayan amiability. For example, someone gives you directions, you say thanks, and they say "Chau! Que pases bien!"

Salado

A multi-use slang word meaning difficult, amazing, enormous, depending on the context. It's literal meaning is salty.

FAAA!

This one just cracks me up. Basically these exclamations are used to express disbelief or astonishment. Kind of like No way! A variation is PAAA!

Tú or vos or usted – which "you" to use in Montevideo?

Montevideans rarely use the formal "usted" unless the person they are speaking to is much older or in a very formal work setting. *Vos* and *tú* are used interchangeably. *Vos* is singular. If you want to say the plural you, use *ustedes*. (*Tú* is virtually never used in Buenos Aires, another indication you are in Montevideo).

If you are interested in Spanish grammar and have not come across *vos* before, here's a little explanation you will find useful.

The verb conjugation for *vos*

The conjugation for *vos* is simpler than for *tú*.
In the present tense, all you do here is drop the final -r from the verb, replace it with an -s ending, and put the accent (and importantly the stress) on the last syllable. That's it. So, *hablar* becomes *vos hablás*, *vivir* becomes *vos vivís*, and *comer* becomes *vos comés*.

Vos and *tú* are used interchangeably but the conjugation is always the *vos* form.

For example, the correct conjugations using the verb "tener" are "tu tienes" and "vos tenés". However, "tienes" is never used in Montevideo. Everyone here would say "tu tenés" or "vos tenés" interchangeably, though of course the *tú* version is grammatically incorrect.

10 Uruguayan films you must see

Uruguayan films typically tend to be slow burners. The action – what little there is of it – unfolds slowly. The lives depicted are monotonous or hard. There is little place for glamour.

If you can't find these films online, once you get to Montevideo, I recommend heading to the gift shop in the Solis Theatre where they have a great selection of Uruguayan films. The English subtitles are generally excellent. One of the translators was also the editor of this very guide.

Whisky (2004)

A dry **tragicomedy**, Whisky revolves around the unspoken relationships between estranged brothers German and Jacobo, and Martha, an employee at Jacobo's decrepit sock factory. The gentle climax of the film take places in the mythical Hotel Argentino in Piriápolis. Probably one of **Uruguay's most well-known** films abroad.

Anina (2013)

After a schoolyard fight, 10-year-old Anina is given the "world's weirdest punishment" – she has to hold onto a wax-sealed black envelope for a week without opening it. What happens if she can't stand the suspense? An absolutely **charming animated children's film** for grown-ups too. If you're wondering, the public school primary school uniform in Uruguay consists of white dustcoats and big blue pussy-cat bows, just like the characters wear.

Mal día para pescar (Bad Day To Go Fishing) (2009)

A washed-up prize-fighter faces his last bout in a backwater town where his only champion in his irrepressible manager. Gorgeously filmed with (uncharacteristically) lots of **drama**.

Hit (2008)

The documentary-makers investigate five Uruguayan hits from 1955 to 1985, including Break it All (sic!), by Uruguay's answer to the Beatles, and a protest song recorded in defiance of the 1970s dictatorship. I adore this film! This is the kind of investigative work that rarely takes place in a country where limited resources mean that social history is rarely documented. You'll notice the younger generations of Uruguayan **musicians** have not heard of the earlier hits.

El Cuarto de Leo (Leo's Room) (2009)

The first Uruguayan film to deal with the issue of **coming out of the closet**. Surprising that it hadn't been tackled earlier. Pictured above.

25 Watts (2001)

Three twenty-something friends hang out in a Montevideo neighbourhood, and as usual, nothing happens. A **cult classic**. Film debut by directors Stoll and Rebella who later went on to film *Whisky*. Fortunately, the sound quality of Uruguayan films has improved hugely since.

El Hombre Nuevo (The New Man) (2015)

Stephania was born a boy in Nicaragua and adopted by a Uruguayan couple during the Sandinista revolution. The film follows Stephania, who watches parked cars for a living, on her journey to rediscover her home country. Aldo Garay's second documentary featuring **transgender** lives.

El baño del Papa (The Pope's Toilet) (2007)

Set in 1987, the Pope will make a visit to a backwoods town in the Uruguayan interior. Many of the locals see it as a once-in-a-lifetime chance to make a fast buck selling food and restroom opportunities (hence the title) to the faithful. **Whimsical** fictional tale.

El viaje hacia el mar (The Trip to the Seaside) (2003)

A band of old guys, most of whom have never seen the sea, despite living less than 100 kilometres from it, are taken by truck to spend the day at the beach. Feel yourself transported back in time and enjoy the scenery on this **gentle**, **humorous** ride.

La Matinee (2007)

A must for **carnival** buffs and culture vultures, the film documents the reforming of a carnival murga by a bunch of old-timers and their younger admirers after years off the boards. Critics have compared the story to Wenders' Buena Vista Social Club.

5 albums to listen to

The Uruguayan music scene has a mixture of rock, pop, tango, folklore, candombe, milonga, carnival sounds. Prepare to be surprised by the creativity and quality of the music emanating from this nation of just three million souls.

Here are five albums that I recommend listening to before you come to visit. While it may be hard to get hold of the albums (even here in Uruguay), you'll be able to find each artist on YouTube.

Jaime Roos – Contraseña (Password)

Jaime, pictured above, is a Uruguayan institution. In a small country like Uruguay, few musicians are able to make a good living from music. Jaime is one of a handful. Forgive him his moustache. He is hugely popular in Uruguay and neighbouring Argentina. This is my favourite album of his, made entirely of versions of songs by other Uruguayan artists. "Amor profundo" (Deep Love) by Mandrake Wolf became a huge hit. What's particularly Uruguayan is the use of carnival *murga* harmonies. The video was shot in Montevideo's Old City. On the album, personally I adore Ney Peraza's guitar on "Tablas". A few years ago Roos branched into cinema, producing a much-loved documentary of a trip his photographer son and he made to South Africa to support Uruguay in the 2010 World Cup called *Tres Millones*.

Mateo – Mateo Solo Bien Se Lame (could be roughly translated as "Mateo does it best alone")

Mateo was a hugely influential songwriter, singer and guitarist emerging in the 1960s. A master of rhythm, he insisted that the nascent rock scene in Uruguay include local candombe-rhythms that were looked down on at the time, leading to the creation of a new rhythm known as candombe-beat. A wildly unpredictable, addictive character who had periods of homelessness, he died penniless before reaching his 50th birthday.

El Principe – El Recital (The Show)

Gustavo Pena, known as El Príncipe (The Prince), also struggled to make a living from music and died in his late 40s just as he was starting to gain popularity and his audiences were beginning to grow. El Recital was recorded live in 2002 with the Club de Tobi. His daughter Eli-U Pena keeps his memory and music alive today, interpreting his songs in her uniquely charismatic style. His poetic lyrics are notable for their positive messages. Like Mateo, El Principe has become a cult musician for musicians in this part of the world.

Ana Prada – Soy Pecadora (I'm a Sinner)

Ana is the modern face of Uruguayan folk music. Her second album is more urban, acoustic with electronic bases, though she continued using folklore rhythms –milonga, valsecito, chamame – as well as reggae. If you are lucky you might get to see Ana play when you are in Montevideo.

Bajofondo – Bajofondo Tango Club

Bajofondo is a Río de la Plata-based music band consisting of eight musicians – four from Uruguay and the other half from Argentina. This is their first album from 2002. The music has been called "electrotango" but the Argentine-Uruguayan influence is more than just tango, and includes murga, milonga and candombe. It's stirring stuff and you'll want more.

Reading

When I was learning Spanish I found that reading books by journalists or short fictional stories was more satisfying than trying to plough through a longer novel or a newspaper. I recommend not stopping every time you don't understand a word, but trying to catch the gist. The first book I ever read in Spanish was *Open Veins of Latin America*, coincidentally by a Uruguayan author, even though I had no idea that years later I would end up in his hometown.

If you want to do a little reading in preparation for your visit, or you are practising your Spanish, I have some recommendations for you.

Recommended titles published in English and Spanish

Eduardo Galeano **"Las Venas Abiertas de América Latina" (Open Veins of Latin America)**
A classic denouncing "five centuries of the pillage of a continent". When it appeared in 1971, it was considered so incendiary that it was banned across South America. It offers you a wealth of historical information in short vignettes. Galeano was a Uruguayan essayist/journalist who was often seen about Montevideo until his death in 2014.

W H Hudson **"The Purple Land" (La tierra purpúrea)**
Available in English and Spanish, Hudson's 1885 chronicle of an Englishman going native in Uruguay was declared the best work of gaucho literature by legendary Argentine author Borges. Hemingway also cites it in The Sun Also Rises. A hugely entertaining read. It was written originally in English.

Eduardo Galeano **"El futbol a sol y sombra"** (Football in Sun and Shadow)
Galeano, as well as being one of Latin America's most eminent progressives, was a huge football fan.

Carolina de Robertis **"The Invisible Mountain"** (La Montaña Invisible)
Written by the daughter of Uruguayan emigres to the US, The Invisible Mountain is one of the few English-language novels you can find set in Uruguay. The book follows three generations of women from 1900 to the turbulent 1960s. An international best-seller nominated for a number of awards.

Recommended titles in Spanish

Here are some recommendations from myself and a wonderful writer, Gabriela Onetto, who kindly put herself in English-speaking shoes to consider the most accessible Uruguayan writers for non-native speakers. You'll have to buy these when you get to Montevideo as they only appear to be available in Spanish.

Mario Benedetti "Montevideanos" and "Con y sin nostalgia"
One of Uruguay's most internationally known writers, Gabriela recommends you focus on his earlier work as his later was rather commercial. His poetry, e.g. "Inventario", is also easy to read as it's like reading someone speaking. If you love him, once you get to Montevideo head to the tourist office and pick up a map that takes you to the different parts of the city linked to his works.

Eleuterio Fernández Huidobro "La fuga de la cárcel de Punta Carretas"
The title translates as The Punta Carretas Jail Break. Current defence minister and ex-Tupamaro guerrilla, Huidobro tells the story of what was in 1971 the world's biggest jail-break when he and 110 other political prisoners tunnelled their way out of the Punta Carretas jail (nowadays a pukka shopping centre) to emerge in the living room of a sympathiser with a house conveniently located next door. Huidobro is a controversial character but there's no getting away from his great narrative style. La Fuga was awarded the Montevideo Municipality Prize in 1990.

For **poetry**, try anything by **Idea Vilariño**, part of the Generation of '45 literary movement and famous for her mythical solitude and intensity.

Newspapers and journals

Uruguay has a bunch of newspapers and weekly journals which are sold from kioskos – stands on the street. If you are learning Spanish and want to practice, to be honest I think that newspapers are generally a difficult source of information. Why? Because they are written for locals and there are many references which are taken for granted which make understanding texts pretty difficult. But if you'd like some recommendations, here goes:

La diaria is Uruguay's only national daily newspaper that is not linked to a political party. It's also a cooperative. It's just 16 pages long and comes out Monday to Friday.

On a Sunday, the most popular paper by far is **El Pais**, principally for its **Gallito** supplement – the classified ads. Good if you're looking for long-term accommodation. El Pais is closely linked to the opposition Nacional Party and is rather conservative and anti-government.

Brecha and **Búsqueda** are weekly journals and both are very dense (content and layout-wise). Brecha is slightly more readable (and has interesting in-depth features) and is more progressive. Búsqueda is more conservative and comes with a glossy magazine. They come out on Thursdays.

Buying books in English in Montevideo

Montevideo has **charming bookshops**. **Más Puro Verso**, Sarandi 675, in the Old City next to the Torres Garcia Museum is probably one of the most **gorgeous**.

The more modern bookshops, especially those in upper-middle-class neighbourhoods like Pocitos and Punta Carretas and in shopping malls, sell a small selection of books in English.

There is a **huge selection of second-hand books in English** at Diomedes Libros on Blvr España 2129 in Parque Rodó.

Acknowledgments

Fernando Alvarez for generously sharing his lovingly-curated database of all the festivals and celebrations in Uruguay and picking out which ones to particularly recommend. He has been running the Fiestas Uruguayas website entirely voluntarily for almost a decade now. The site is visited by tens of thousands of Uruguayans primarily from the interior.

Diego Lopez at Carnaval del Uruguay for providing the only source of up-to-date information about Montevideo carnival, also without official or commercial support.

Uruguay produces more architects per capita than most other countries. And they are formidably trained. When I lived in Buenos Aires, it felt like all my friends were psychoanalysts. Here in Montevideo all my friends are architects. I am grateful to two – **Silvia Andrada** and **Susana Ardemagni** – in particular for allowing me to pick their brains for architectural gems.

I have run to **Rossana Demarco** of La Pasionaria many times over the years for her sage advice on art and design in Montevideo. Thanks, Rossana, for sharing your hard-earned insight and information about art galleries and museums.

My long-time friend, **Alicia Fernandez**, who I met the year I arrived in Montevideo, 2000. Our kids were in the same class for virtually their entire schooling. Alice started dancing tango in her fifties and is a regular at Montevideo milongas. I am indebted for her insider advice on the best places to go tango in Montevideo. Thanks to **Casa Sarandi guests** who dance tango and explained the very real differences between the milonga environments in Buenos Aires versus Montevideo.

Carolina at Friendly Point for her advice on gay Montevideo and to **Rodrigo Borda** for putting me in contact with her.

Being a beer woman, I could never have written the two wonderful chapters on wine and section on Shopping for wine-lovers. So I am indebted to **Viviana del Rio** of Bodegas del Uruguay, the only Spanish-language website exclusively dedicated to Uruguayan wines. Viviana and her Bodegas co-founder **Claudio Angelotti** organise VinoSub30, a competition encouraging high-level wine-expertise in the under-30s.

Carolina Barrios at JSB Tourism for her help with information about travel to Iguazú and to **Pity Mascaro** for suggesting I contact her, and to the folks at Free Uruguay Expats for additional travel tips.

One of my favourite chapters in this guide is the rather personal one on the history of Uruguay and how it has affected what you as visitors see when you come to Montevideo. For providing answers to the questions I had, huge thanks to historian **Aldo Marchesi**, brother of my friend Ani, who so distressed the would-be robber in the Uruguayan Character chapter. Aldo is a regular face on national TV so our conversation which took place in Carrera, a classic cafe in the city centre attracted the attention of a little old lady who asked if she could listen in, and then leaning on her shopping trolley, proceeded to add to Aldo's responses as well as tell him that he should make sure he got well-remunerated for his information.

Uruguayan writer **Gabriela Onetto** kindly put herself in English-speaking shoes to consider the most accessible Uruguayan writers for non-native speakers as featured in the Reading chapter.

My son **Ivan** for knocking around music (and other) recommendations with me until they would take on a form that I was happy with.

Erika Bernhardt for her work on the Guru'Guay logo and the **Montevideo Government** for making the Torres Garcia font used for the title of this book freely available for public use.

Angela McCallum of San Telmo Loft in Argentina by way of New Orleans for her inspiration and generosity sharing knowledge on website and graphic design. Angela, you've shortened the learning curve a number of times.

Lori "Eagle Eye" Nordstrom for proofreading this guide – and often informally my blog posts.

I am indebted to all the photographers who share their work on Flickr.com and particularly to **Jimmy Baikovicius** who every time I do a search on Uruguay has added something new and wildly beautiful to his photography collection. I still cannot believe his stormy photo of the rambla.

The people that inhabit the Facebook group formerly known as **Uruguay Free Expats** (now Uruguay Expat Community) are a generous resource and I am always grateful for their feedback and suggestions.

My friends especially those living in Uruguay regularly get grilled for tidbits that end up in some shape or form on Guru'Guay. I hope I have not ruined too many secret spots.

All the guests over the years at Casa Sarandi Guesthouse, particularly **Thorsten Petter** from Germany who insisted that I really should turn our little four-page guide to Montevideo into a website. And **Rachel, Yvonne, Jaik and Brett**, the first-ever guests. Look at what you started.

My old friend from Birmingham University, **Lesley Davies-Evans**, for coming up with the brilliant moniker, Guru'Guay. It still makes me laugh. (And to **Piet Bess** whose Guay-not was a close runner-up.) And of course, thank you to my partner **Sergio** –"the man behind the Guru" – with whom I started Casa Sarandi in 2010.

Photography credits

I am very grateful to the photographers, many of them professional, who share their wonderful work on Flickr.com. Thank you to you all for your generosity and for helping bring Montevideo to life for the readers of this guide.

Introduction   Jimmy Baikovicius Montevideo skyline at night

Weather   Vince Alongi Montevideo skyline at sunset

When to visit   Jimmy Baikovicius Young Uruguayan football supporter

Holidays and festivals   Jimmy Baikovicius Iemanjá Sea Goddess celebrations

Where to stay   Jimmy Baikovicius People eating in the Cafe Bacacay in the Ciudad Vieja, the rambla in Punta Carretas, Hotel Sofitel which dominates the Carrasco rambla, the Plaza del Entrevero in Centro, the rambla in Parque Rodó

Accommodation   Jimmy Baikovicius Hotel Sofitel which dominates the Carrasco rambla

Public transport   Jimmy Baikovicius Scene in a Montevideo taxi

Driving   Jimmy Baikovicius Ford Taurus 1957

Communicating   A K Mahan, Children using free XOs

Exchanging money   Bryan Mason "I'm a millionaire"

Architecture   Nicolas Barreiro Dupuy The Old Jockey Club of Montevideo; Jimmy Baikovicius Puertito de Buceo

Museums   Karen A Higgs, Gaucho Museum staircase

Art galleries   Karen A Higgs, Painting by Blanes

Historic cafes and bars   Karen A Higgs, Clube Brasileiro

Beaches   kumsval, Montevideo (Playa Ramirez); Jimmy Baikovicius Puertito de Buceo

Outdoors   Karen A Higgs, Botanical Gardens in El Prado

Tours   Karen A Higgs, Murga in Montevideo Carnival

Day trips   Jimmy Baikovicius Isla Gorriti in Punta del Este

Shopping   kweez mcG Mates for sale in the ferias

Carnival   Karen A Higgs, Murga

Tango milongas   Embajada de los Estados Unidos en Uruguay Tango dancing

Bands to see live   Jimmy Baikovicius Nicolas Arnicho, percussionist

Live music venues   Cristian Menghi Ana Prada

Gay Montevideo   Jimmy Baikovicius "Montevideo" gets a paint-over

Time locals eat   Christian Córdova Clock in the Port Market

Food   Jimmy Baikovicius Torta frita

Restaurants   Jimmy Baikovicius Parrillero in the Port Market; Karen A Higgs, Dessert at Foc; Brian Fitzharris Parrillero in the Port Market

Breakfast   Karen A Higgs, Candy Bar

History   Karen A Higgs, Farewell to President Pepe Mujica 2015

Films   Enrique Buchichio, Still from "Leo's Room"

Albums   Jimmy Baikovicius Jaime Roos

Reading   Antoine Hubert Más Puro Verso bookshop in Ciudad Vieja

Final words

Guru'Guay and the Guru'Guay Guides are an independent initiative
run by me, a Welsh woman, from my home in Montevideo
where I've been living since 2000.

If you found them useful, I'd encourage you to help make this labour of pure love
possible by recommending to your friends.

The Guru'Guay Guide to Montevideo is Guru'Guay's first publication.
In 2016 I will be working on *The Guru'Guay Guide to Uruguay*.

Looking forward to helping make your stay in
Montevideo and Uruguay really, really memorable.

Karen Higgs, aka "The Guru"

PS. I'd love to hear from you.
See you on www.guruguay.com
Facebook www.facebook.com/Guruguay1
or Twitter www.twitter.com/GuruGuay1

Made in the USA
Middletown, DE
04 July 2016